"EVEN A FLOWER..."

A Memoir on Emotional Integrity and Spiritual Breadwinning

Adam Elliot

"Even A Flower..."
A Memoir on Emotional Integrity and
Spiritual Breadwinning

Perach Press, an imprint of
Adam Elliot, Publishers

For information about volume discounts
or author appearances,
address the publisher at:

4730 E. Indian School Rd.
Suite 120-150
Phoenix, AZ 85018
or
evenaflower@aol.com

ISBN: 0-9722498-0-X

Printed in the United States of America

*To every heart so foolish
as to have no doubt, and
to every mind so arrogant
as to have no faith.*

Contents

PART ONE

SENSATION

Midrash (Allegory) For Part One:
Adam and Eve's Daring Gambit

When God first envisioned a physical world, *sensation* was what came to Mind. Seeing, hearing, feeling, smelling and tasting. A network of neuroreceptors, hardwired to know light from dark, hot from cold, not-enough from too-much. The idea of consciousness ensconced in matter was a big bang indeed.

What God did not foresee was physicality's potential as a medium for *relation*. It was Adam (on the ground) who conceived of an interpersonal operating system for the sensory mainframe. He asked for and was granted a companion. And there were *two* human prototypes, enjoying the fruits of the Garden.

It takes one for sensation; two for relation. But there was evening and there was morning . . . and Eve seemed redundant. Adam's sight and touch confirmed that like everything else the Lord had made, she, too, "was good." But her physical attributes did little to assuage his relational malaise.

"There's no such *thing* as loneliness," the serpent chided Adam. "It's all in your oversized, *homo sapiens* head!" Indeed, in all creation, only Eve shared the quintessentially human instinct—even in physical paradise—to gird sensation with relation. "I feel it too," she whispered. "Something's missing."

Eve knew this without needing to eat from the Tree of Knowledge. She was clear from the outset she'd not embodied for sensation. She wanted to *interact*. To express, in and through the physical, her *extra*-sensory, image-of-God Essence.

But relation couldn't manifest, like the human genome, on a mere word from the Creator. Adam and Eve would have to work at this. To make their incipient feelings flesh. And keep on breathing life into them.

As if that weren't challenge enough for two newborns, their communicative agenda was beset, from the beginning, with a paradox: Eden's very abundance made it functionally obsolescent the moment relation was thought of. For the essence of relation is the will to share. But in the Garden, Adam and Eve already *had* everything. And only God (not each other) to thank.

That's why Adam had to give up paradise and get a job. He wanted to "bring home the bacon." So he could *share* it . . . with his beloved.

Introduction

Are We "Irretrievably Broken"?

In my generation, 25 years is a long time to be married to the same person. At the synagogue where I chant blessings for people celebrating milestone events, the most recent *"misheberach"** was for a 56th anniversary (after which the husband quipped, "and she's lucky to *have* me!"). But fewer and fewer of us are managing to hold our relationships together. It's reached the point several states are reconsidering no-fault divorce, the now almost universal approach that allows either spouse to terminate the marriage whenever he or she has had enough.

On August 9, 1995, Diane and I would have celebrated our 25th anniversary. But we separated in June. There may have been a few prayers for us during this time, but no anniversary *misheberachs*.

The central allegation in a divorce petition is that the marriage is "irretrievably broken." Recent events surely make that case for ours. Yet we still claim to love each other. Both the lawyer and the optimist in me thus keep

---

*A prayer, usually for health, which begins, *"Misheberach avotey-nu"*—"May He who blessed our ancestors, Abraham, Isaac, and Jacob..."

5

railing against that word "irretrievably." And that other word . . . "love."

If one of us had died, *that* would have made things irretrievable. But since we've survived, at least physically, how can I give up on a marriage we've both put so much into . . . and on which our three sons are still so dependent?

So I'm amending the divorce petition to read:

> *Certain differences **that may prove to be** irreconcilable have arisen between the parties, for whom the future holds a variety of possibilities ranging from reconciliation to divorce. Having initiated this action for dissolution, Adam now requests that it be treated as a petition for legal separation.*

Dire as our marital circumstances may be, I want to believe things can still be turned around. I'm aware this could be a case of massive denial. The amount of water under our bridge makes the very thought of reconciliation neurotically suspect—a refusal to see the obvious. Or, as my dad would have said, to "tell it like it is."

But my father was a cynic, whereas I profess to be both psychologically and *spiritually* committed. What shall those twin faiths mean for me in the current crisis? That I'm walking my spiritual talk . . . or just grasping at straws? And if it's the latter, is that bad or good? Under present circumstances, is "reality" worth the price?

There's a prayer we recite each Sabbath as we stand before the Holy Ark: *"Bey, bey, bey ana racheytz"*—"Not in any man, prophet or intercessor do we put our trust, but only in God Himself." This ancient Aramaic, dating to the time of Jesus, is sung in a haunting, minor key. I've always been drawn to the melody and remember singing it, somewhat guiltily, to my infant sons.

For our marriage has been on death's door before, and we've entrusted it to spiritual as well as psychological intercessors. Somehow, their quackish ministrations brought us into a behavioral remission. But a decade later, the malady has metastasized, throwing us into a crisis of faith as well as emotion.

How did we get here? For twenty-five years, we've been retracing our steps, trying to find our way *back* to the Garden of Eden. It didn't take me many years of working for a living to realize I wanted back there. I'd long assumed Diane/Eve had similarly reconsidered her commitment to life in the relational wilderness.

Recent events suggest, however, that if I'm serious about returning to the Garden, I may have to go there alone . . . or with somebody else.

1

The Boy in the Ark

In the beginning, the terms of my relationship with God were clear. My job was to behave; His, to make sure only good things happened to my family and me. The arrangement was so simple (and personal), I even gave Him a nickname—an acronym of all our first initials.

Our synagogue, B'nai Israel, was a grand and mysterious place that went well with my childish theology. Just inside the Negley Avenue entrance, a tunnel-like corridor wound steeply around the sanctuary's perimeter. Its curved slope connoted an ascending pilgrimage, especially for those with little or tired old legs.

At the summit, one came into a cavernous hall, with a high, domed ceiling. Chandeliers in the shape of giant Stars of David twinkled brightly. Down a long center aisle, the rich mahogany Ark, resplendent with gold-painted lions, rose up 25 feet from the dais. And hidden behind its sliding wooden doors, then a sheer white curtain, were the sacred Torah scrolls, each ornately garbed and crowned.*

*Each scroll contains the first five books of the Bible, handwritten on parchment.

Once, around age nine, I sneaked into the darkened sanctuary. It was a spooky scene, the only light being the red *Ner Tamid* (Eternal Light) that hung above the Ark. Standing in that awesome space, I wondered what would happen were I to steal a bit farther . . . right up into the Ark itself! Might I then feel like one of God's own Torah scrolls, holy and beloved?

On Saturday mornings, the choir sang from a loft, so high up it evoked an angelic presence. They accompanied the Cantor,* who pled our case with high notes so vigorous they turned his whole face red. Yet when the liturgical mood shifted, he could also beseech God in a sacred falsetto whisper.

We rose to our feet when the Ark was finally opened. As the Cantor reached in to remove one of the Torahs, its silver crown and breastplate jangled in anticipation of the excursion down into the hubbub of the congregation. *"Ki mitziyon teytzey Torah,"* sang the choir—"Out of Zion shall go forth the Law." The Cantor then led a procession around the sanctuary, pausing for those who wished to kiss the Torah . . . and singing majestically all the while.

His voice was my Pied Piper. When I was old enough to take my place in the celestial choir loft, the first thing I had to learn was how to funnel so large an exuberance into just the small sound I was trying to emit. Sometimes, it was all I could do to mouth the words.

---

*In traditional congregations, the cantor leads the worship service, chanting the prayers, in Hebrew.

Singing was thus my first love, but also the source of my earliest disillusionment. All too soon, it was clear that my vocal reach exceeded my grasp. The solos were going to other members of the youth choir. Then, as my Bar Mitzvah approached, my voice began cracking, unpredictably.

God smiled on me that day, and I made it through in rare form. It was as though I'd been granted a boon—one opportunity to sing decently and uninhibitedly before the axe fell. Thereafter, my adolescent "gap" continued to widen, to the point I simply couldn't produce anything remotely resembling a well-placed tone.

In our high school choir, I distinguished myself not as singer but as student conductor. I went so far as to take an aptitude test at a local conservatory. The scoring sheet confirmed my facility for pitch, rhythm and such. But the fine print cautioned that first and foremost, an aspiring musician must show distinct vocal or instrumental promise. Someone had placed three asterisks beside the admonition (as if I might have missed it).

At age 17, I went off to Israel. Something I'd said or written had called me to the attention of the Dean of the College of Jewish Studies, on whose recommendation I received a scholarship for a year's study in Jerusalem. On my return, now fluent in Hebrew, I enrolled in a cantorial workshop, offered by the Hebrew Union College.

The class met for three hours each Tuesday night, at the synagogue of the cantor-instructor. How strange to see the elaborate prayer modes written out, note for note, with English transliteration. I was hooked on this immediately and had little difficulty mastering the material from a musical or linguistic standpoint. But the karma encrypted on my vocal cords proved immune to perseverance.

Resignedly, I enrolled at Purdue, with a major in political science. I nevertheless inflicted myself on the school's *a cappella* choir and even experimented with a voice class. After a willful semester of vocal calisthenics, I ended up with a "C" in the course (not the tenor high C to which I so aspired). When I protested that I'd diligently done everything the instructor had asked of me, his response was, "Yes, I know; but *you* didn't improve."

My efforts did win me the opportunity to help a new congregation get started, serving as its part-time cantor. I did this for a few years, while attending law school—then gave it up to pursue my second choice for a career.

Law school turned out to be an exhilarating experience, particularly in comparison to my undergraduate, liberal arts courses. Here, at last, was a subject matter that truly mattered. The fate of the disputants turned on how we reconciled opposing principles and conflicting social agendas.

I found this a most satisfying integration of abstract reasoning and day-to-day practicality. Unlike my classmates, who mostly took the curriculum as a kind of hazing they had to endure (until they could begin earning their living as attorneys), I actually enjoyed the law. For me, it was the transition to earning a living that would pose the real challenge.

This was complicated by the fact that I'd begun exploring spiritual life in formats totally alien to my Jewish upbringing. It began when one of the lawyers at the firm where I was doing my summer clerking invited me along to his regular, Sunday morning yoga lesson. The class was taught, ironically enough, by a religiously observant Jewish woman who happened to have her own hatha yoga studio.

On the surface, hatha yoga is a physical discipline, consisting of a series of postures, held with a high degree of concentration. But more than my spine was flexing and relaxing. With each long, measured breath, my cluttered psyche was unlimbering. By the end of that first hour and a half session, I was in a wonderfully calm but alert state I hadn't experienced before. So I continued with my own weekly yoga lessons for the next year or so.

In my third year of law school, I was able to enjoy a respite from the competitiveness of the first two years. On the strength of my performance as a law clerk, the firm had guaranteed me a position after graduation. I thus was spared the rigors of job seeking with which my classmates were contending. The curriculum itself was less demanding, and with my immediate future secure, maintaining a high class standing seemed considerably less urgent.

It was during this happy time that I found myself reading *Autobiography of a Yogi,* by Parmahansa Yogananda. In the life story of this inspired swami, I found an exotic yet vaguely familiar approach to God and religion. Had I not known such reverence myself, years before? Yogananda's writing reminded me of the boy who had wanted to be a Torah scroll. And made me wonder where that child had gone . . . why he'd not progressed to a more mature but no less vital spiritual awareness.

Adolescence, it seems, had disrupted more than my vocal registers. There was now a disconnect between my intellect and the ceremony that had once so moved me. Judaism, to be sure, was no less rich in religious symbolism (and ethical substance). But my own inner shine—what our sacred objects merely reflect back to us—seemed to have tarnished. A phrase from the Sabbath prayer book comes to mind: *"Chadeysh yameynu kekedem"*—"Renew our days as of old."

My alienation may indeed have reflected a more widespread Jewish malaise. In the fifties and sixties, we were still reeling from the shock of the Holocaust. It's not surprising, at such point in our long history, that personal communion with God (which seemed not to have availed the six million) should have taken a back seat to a more sectarian, less spiritual religious life. The champions of our physical survival were the Zionists. But for most American Jews, whose security militated against emigration to Israel, preservation of the religious culture (what we now call "Jewish continuity") came to be viewed as an end in itself.

But Jewish peoplehood couldn't assuage an emerging generation's more elemental need for faith in God. At this equally critical stage of our personal development, our religious mentors seemed not really to want the job. So when, in typical adolescent fashion, we challenged their theology, they pulled the rug right out from under us: "Fine. How very bright of you to be skeptical. We now ordain *you* the leaders of the religious community!"

In this way, my generation was like the four sons we

read of in the Passover *Haggadah:** At first, too young to question; then just capable of rote learning. For a time, we asked, sincerely, what all the ceremony was about. But as our social and intellectual development seemed only to distance us from the purported Object of our ritual practices, our disillusionment fell on deaf ears. Almost inevitably, we became the rebellious child, who asks, provocatively, "What are *you* getting out of all this religious mumbo jumbo?"

If the Orthodox measure of Jewish living was the dutiful performance of *mitzvot* (religious commandments), for the less observant majority, it was Jewish charitable work or communal activity (usually centered around support for the State of Israel). Jewish leadership fell to those who could articulate the "Jewish point of view" on a given subject—with poise, verbal clarity and mental conviction. Like good lawyers, in short. But neither the curriculum nor the modeling informed of a direct, personal or life-influencing relationship with God.

I know even as I write such a phrase that it will make many Jews cringe, connoting something alien to our mainstream Jewish culture. This, I think, makes my very point. In spite of our post-Emancipation discomfort with such a notion, pious Jews from Abraham forward have had, at the center of their identities, just such a relationship with (or at least a yearning for) *"Hashem."***

*The manual that sets out the ritual for the Passover meal.

**Hebrew for the unspeakable name of God.

Now here in my third year of law school, I had all the qualifications to take my place as an active, indeed prominent member of the adult Jewish community. I had the birthright and the education. I could articulate Rabbi Kaplan's* theory of God as "the Power that makes for salvation"—even if I couldn't apply it in any personally useful way. What I hadn't learned from my Judaic curriculum was how to experience a sense of relationship with my Creator.

But some ancient signal, apperceived by the young boy standing in awe before the Holy Ark, now flickered again, like a personal *Ner Tamid*. And for the moment, Swami Yogananda was its unlikely custodian.

*Mordechai Kaplan, founder of the Reconstructionist branch of Judaism.

2

Signs and Wonders

Yogananda stressed that it was possible to know God experientially, not just metaphorically. I'd seen this in tracts handed out by missionaries of various stripe (which I'd dismissed as so much self-delusion on their part). Perhaps what was different about Yogananda's message was that he was telling the story of his own life, not threatening me with eternal damnation. In all events, my circumstances now allowed me the time and energy for some spiritual experimentation.

One day, after an hour or so of yoga postures and deep breathing, I felt particularly alert and focused. "Why not give it a try?" I asked myself. "Give what a try?" I answered. "You know, the talking to *God* thing."

Since no one was looking, I allowed myself, just barely, to continue along these lines. I did some more deep breathing and found my attention gathered at the spot between the eyebrows, sometimes called the "third eye." I fancied myself putting out a signal-beam to God's 1-800 number: "Okay, I'm here. I'm skeptical. (In fact, if ever asked, I'll probably deny we *had* this conversation.) But if You're there and willing to make contact, I'd welcome some response."

Yogananda, I remembered, had a guru to help him make the divine connection. Indeed, he had seen the face of his spiritual teacher in meditation before meeting him in the flesh. Willing to settle for such a sign, I began conjuring up visages of current-day holy people, whose names I'd seen on placards or in books.

"What if asking for this kind of thing (or even 'being open to it') means I've already *half lost my mind?"* I panicked. "Oh, give it a rest," some more adventuresome part of me prodded. "You'll either get some kind of response or you won't."

Pressing ahead, I tried to visualize someone walking toward me—an item of clothing or some unique ornament by which I might later recognize my spiritual teacher. The image came to mind of a large red flower.

After half an hour or so, it occurred to me that this was the first real praying I had done since my childhood, in the sense of directing a message to God while entertaining the possibility He might actually hear and respond. I was skeptical, but I was doing it. Not as a ritual and not for public consumption. As some Christians might have put it, I was "knocking."

It also seemed clear that the images passing through my mind during this prayer-meditation were products of my own invention. In fact, I got up from the exercise rather disappointed that nothing whatever had been accomplished.

That evening, I stopped by a relative's house where a distant cousin was visiting from England. I had no other information about him and no particular expectations for the encounter. But I soon learned it was no mere holiday that had brought Cousin Jeff to America. He'd come all this way to attend a "festival," at the Houston Astrodome . . . with a fourteen year old *guru* named Deva Ji!

I'd seen this kid's picture on posters near the Purdue campus. In fact, he was one of the guru-candidates I'd thought of during my meditation! Six hours later, my hitherto unknown cousin was commending him to me, in terms Yogananda himself might have used: the current *Sat-guru* (true teacher)—whose very job was to open my inner eye . . . so that I might know God *for myself.*

"I'm not proposing you *believe* in Gurudeva Ji," Jeff pitched me almost irresistibly. "Just give him a chance to show you what he can do. He'll either deliver or he won't."

With the benefit of a quarter-century's hindsight, I can picture God (or an administrative assistant) fielding my call: "What are we going to do for *this* poor guy?" They may have looked quickly around the neighborhood, spotting Gurudeva Ji in Houston and Cousin Jeff, with his lay-over in Chicago. "This is the best we can come up with on short notice; let's just see what he'll do with it."

Though more than a little intrigued, I never mentioned my meditation earlier in the day nor gave Jeff any inkling what a hot prospect he'd stumbled upon. As I was leaving, he handed me a magazine about the guru to take home. I tossed it onto my coffee table, and it was a day or two before I gave the encounter with my cousin much further thought.

I'm sure I wasn't meditating or otherwise spiritually exerting myself as I sat there on my couch that day. But something drew my attention, almost magnetically, to the picture on the magazine's cover. I felt my head rotate slightly to the left, as though of its own accord. Just enough for my gaze to fall upon the gaudy *red flower* leaping out at me from the guru's lapel!

Now in twenty some years of attending religious services and reciting rote prayers, I'd never had such an experience. Word of other people's cosmic encounters with Gurudeva Ji added fuel to my fire, and in short order, I, too, was singing his praises.

But the notion of an exalted *Satguru* troubled me. This was the early '70s, and the Jesus freaks, "est"-people and followers of myriad *babas* and *anandas* (often themselves former Epsteins and Moskowitzes) had signs and wonders of their own. It was as though there were three types of people in the world: skeptics, those who had found God and those who only thought they had found Him. (And of course, the latter only made it harder for those of us in the middle category to get through to those in the first.)

Nevertheless, I continued to have extraordinary experiences that reinforced my allegiance to the guru. While practicing a meditation technique called "listening to the music," strains of a Renaissance motet wafted ethereally through my right ear! The sound was so vivid, I barely made it through the first stanza before jumping up to make certain no one had a radio on in the adjacent room. (There was no radio, but after the unscheduled intermission, no more motet.)

Another time, I became immersed in something I can only relate to the phrase "filled with the Holy Spirit." I called Diane into the little, darkened hallway I used for meditation and tried to describe what I was feeling. But the sensation only quickened, outstripping any thought of running commentary. This time, it seemed right to give the experience my undivided attention, and Diane (assessing me no danger to myself or others) graciously excused me to whatever I was in the throes of.

This meditation had the feel of a tutorial—some precognitive colloquy that rose, as I tuned in, to an inspired height. I exulted there some inchoate while. And then, like the parting kiss of a spiritual lover, my reverie came into more prosaic focus.

I was a public defender at the time, and the upshot was a new perspective on my clients (indigent criminal defendants), on one hand, and those presiding over their due process, on the other. I tried to capture the idea part of this in a poem:

Paragons and Miscreants

Our paragons and miscreants were cut from selfsame cloth.
And equally enfranchised in the only mortal business—
that of getting (or of staying)
just as comfortable as circumstance permits.

By dint of jurisprudence drafted by my well placed peers,
our livelihood seems honest and secure.
My clients, though, must answer
for desires we can satisfy but they can ill afford.

And for us, a nonpecuniary perk:
We're seen all the more upstanding for our salutary work.
Our pride and joy; their due process . . .
All men are berated equal.

Whatever the above evokes, there was no trace of cynicism or self-reproach in the experience itself. No polemic against lawyers or some power elite, the essence of the epiphany was its very objectivity. Crowning of a bright, non-verbal piece, it was awareness, not thought—a beholding: of the ultimate innocence of every human being, however derelict his behavior.

I'm sure many people can look back on their lives and recall singular moments they felt in touch with the Divine. These may be associated with the early stage of one spiritual path or another. I heard a priest, once, reflecting on the visitations that first called him to the priesthood. Now nearer the end of his vocation, he shared this wise hindsight: "Our spiritual life cannot subsist on exotic visions we may be graced to see or feel. So should you chance upon a burning bush, receive it as a sacramental boon. But then, as Moses did, get on about your Father's work. Lest *un*called for mystic pining obscure, rather than illumine, your earthly path."

Lacking all such maturity, I started ranking my meditations. Then, just as fast as enlightenment had struck, I seemed to lose the meditative knack. For a while, I thought this must be some kind of test—why else would God have just stopped showing up? In my youthful ardor, it seemed fair, not contradictory, that the extraordinary (now that I'd validated its existence) should consign itself to my meditative beck and call.

Soon enough, though, the press of my own worldly business had me wondering how many hours of meditation a riff of monaural music was really worth. At the risk of getting further ahead of myself, my thought today is, not very many! Perhaps the special effects were provided, in the beginning, as a kind of spiritual Welcome Wagon. After which I was being called more and more, not less and less . . . to notice the miraculous in my everyday life and interactions.

I eventually made grudging peace with the inconsistency of my meditational experience and took my spiritual pleasures where I found them. For example, I was told during my initiation ceremony that if I ever got near enough to Guradeva Ji, I should cup my right ear and ask him for "holy breath." With that in mind, I positioned myself outside the rear entrance of a hall where the guru was speaking, hoping to catch him on his way out.

"Gurudeva Ji, could I have holy breath?" I petitioned, as he came bounding toward me. The guru grabbed me affectionately around the shoulders. Then, curling the fingers of his other hand to form a tube, he gave a quick blow into my right ear. At that instant, I felt a corkscrew like penetration—not of air, but of some unknown medium. It was strangely nonphysical, though it did seem to enter through the ear.

Once again, the sensation was so vivid, it seems pointless to quibble over its reality (whatever I may now make of its significance). Certainly, I'd been "programmed" to expect something cosmic, but what does that really explain? If a faith healer exhorts someone into a suggestible state, does that make the ensuing experience any less real? Looking back with this perspective, I've no good explanation for holy breath (or other phenomena we experienced as devotees of Gurudeva Ji).

Nor for a similar episode with Diane, long before I'd begun testing any spiritual waters. When she first told me she loved me, her *statement* had the same kind of penetrating effect—that time, a slicing (not spiraling), into the center of my chest. As with holy breath, it wasn't uncomfortable; just vivid, and completely out of the ordinary.

Our young marriage was severely tested, however, when I became a devotee of Gurudeva Ji. For though I've focused here on a few sensational experiences, it was the subtler but more consistent quality of devotion emanating from the guru's followers (but not my wife) that was winning my spiritual heart.

These were people of all ages, some children and some in their eighties, who would step to the front of the room and extemporaneously express their love for God in the most personal and eloquent way. There were no agendas, scripts or cue cards for these nightly *satsang** programs. Only those who felt moved to speak came forward, and no one rushed to fill the occasional meditative hiatus.

I found the inspiration and sense of well-being at *satsang* so intoxicating, I soon was taking pains to get there for my nightly fix. Needless to say, our home life was profoundly affected by this dependency . . . and by my absence.

Diane had just completed her masters degree and taken a job as a family and child therapist. She'd also started into her own psychoanalysis. Her professional and personal

---

*Sanskrit for "company of truth" or "holy discourse."

lives were thus orienting her 180 degrees from the direction life was taking me.

I don't recall the exchange that finally brought things to a head, but I ended up packing my bags and taking an apartment not far from my office. I shared this space with a "blissed out" but utterly derelict devotee, whose previous address had been the woods across from Deva Ji's ashram. My separation from Diane didn't last more than a few weeks, however, and our reconciliation was triggered by another divine intervention I credited to the guru.

My car was in the shop, and I'd been sitting in the customers' lounge, reading *The Aquarian Gospel*. This book was popular among the devotees, but I couldn't seem to concentrate on it. Diane and I hadn't spoken for about a week, and my mind kept wandering to that situation. Should I call her? Should I wait for her to call me?

I paced a number of times to the pay phone on the wall. Then, a rather authoritative thought occurred to me. "READ THE NEXT CHAPTER OF THE BOOK BEFORE YOU DECIDE." I sat back down, opened to exactly where I had left off, and this is what I found:

Chapter 77
Jesus in Hebron. Goes to Bethany.
Advises Ruth Regarding Certain
Family Troubles.

* * *

The evening came; the multitudes were gone, and Jesus, Lazarus and his sisters, Martha, Ruth and Mary, were alone. And Ruth was sore distressed. Her home was down in Jericho; her husband was the keeper of an inn; his name was Asher-ben.

Now, Asher was a Pharisee of strictest mien and thought, and he regarded Jesus with disdain.

And when his wife confessed her faith in Christ, he drove her from his home.

But Ruth resisted not; she said, "If Jesus is the Christ, He knows the way, and I am sure he is the Christ."

"My husband may become enraged and slay my human form; he cannot kill the soul, and in the many mansions of my Fatherland, I have a dwelling-place."

*And Ruth told Jesus all; and then she said, "**What shall I do?***"*

***And Jesus said:** "Your husband is not willingly at fault; he is devout. He prays to God, our Father-God.*

He feels assured that he has done the will of God in driving you away.

Intolerance is ignorance matured.

The light will come to him someday, and then he will repay for all your heartaches, griefs and tears.

And Ruth, you must not think that you are free from blame.

If you had walked in wisdom's ways and been content to hold your peace, this grief would not have come to you."

"It takes a long, long time for light to break into the shell of prejudice, and patience is the lesson you have need to learn.

The constant dropping of the water wears away the hardest stone.

The sweet and holy incense of a godly life will melt intolerance much quicker than the hottest flame or hardest blow.

Just wait a little time and then go home, with sympathy and love. Talk not of Christ nor of the kingdom of the Holy One.

Just live a godly life, refrain from harshness in your speech, and you will lead your husband to the light."

And it was so. *

Decades later, I can hardly read this text without getting a lump in my throat. Diane was as ensconced as any Pharisee in her psychoanalytic religion. Her concern for my well-being was sincere. But like Ruth's husband, she'd grown intolerant of my heresy.

However skeptical any reader may be about this incident—convinced that I'd subliminally glimpsed the next chapter-heading and used it as a means of resolving my ambivalence about calling Diane—I ask you to give at least my sincerity (or naivete) the benefit of the doubt. Can you

*Reprinted by permission of De Vorss Publications, from *The Aquarian Gospel of Jesus the Christ*, by Levi.

imagine what it meant to me to think the guru was now interceding in my marital behalf?

I did phone Diane, and we got together about an hour later. But quite contrary to the counsel Jesus gave Ruth, I heard myself extolling Deva Ji, yet again, to my long suffering wife. Some trance-like *satsang* poured out of me for five, seamless minutes.

Yet this time, Diane was taken (not turned off) by the onslaught. When I finally stopped speaking, she declared she could no longer deny her attraction to whatever was so moving me . . . or her desire to experience it herself!

I'm reminded here of the scene in *When Harry Met Sally,* where Meg Ryan fakes an orgasm in the restaurant to prove to Billy Crystal she's not sexually repressed. A woman at the next table tells the waitress, "I'll have whatever *she's* having."

So was this all some kind of spiritual masturbation? Was any part of it real? Or was it, like Meg Ryan's performance, an audacious prank? (And if so, *who* was the prankster?)

Diane did let me "lead her to the light," and she, too, had some memorable experiences as a devotee. But whatever spell Gurudeva Ji and I had cast on her soon began to wear off. As our relationship again deteriorated, that reversal added inexorably to my own growing doubts about the guru.

These had to do with the increasingly unrealistic burden of daily meditation (two hours for serious devotees) and nightly *satsang* of equal length; additional gatherings, wherever and whenever Deva Ji called them (like the one Cousin Jeff had come all the way from England to attend);

and incessant appeals to buy the guru another car, house or helicopter!

Then at *satsang,* one evening, they rolled out Deva Ji's new look. Our erstwhile guru would continue to make occasional public appearances (and, presumably, to accept donations). But no longer was he on a mission from God. There would be no more holy breath; no more pilgrimages to his "lotus feet;" and no more nightly *satsang.*

Deva Ji, come to find out, was a fairly ordinary young man, with some meditation techniques. The whole personality cult had been "imposed" on him by his now too parochial Indian flock. And, apparently, his own mother . . . at whose urging, back in the old country, the faithful were now flocking to the lotus feet of her more doting son, Megaditto Ji.

On hearing the above, I felt called to address my fellow devotees in a manner that was anything but trance-like. "As far as I'm concerned," I declared, "Deva Ji can carry on as *Satguru* and let the world keep right on calling him a con artist. Or he can retire comfortably and prove the world right!"

"*Satguru* or con artist—he surely doesn't qualify for anything in between."

3

Sarah

My condition in the late '70s and early '80s was one of severe disillusionment, not knowing what to make of the above experiences and trying to limp along without a sense of spiritual direction. I'd left the large law firm after only a year and become a deputy public defender for Cook County. Schizophrenic as my professional and devotional responsibilities had made me during that first year in private practice, I found it impossible even to feign meditative equanimity in the frenzied environment of the Public Defender's Office. So after three hectic years there, I took refuge in a position at Loyola Law School, teaching legal research and writing to first-year students.

At Loyola, I struck up a friendship with a faculty member who, on learning of my spiritual search, confided that he himself was working with a psychic healer. For a while, I resisted his offer to introduce me to her, but my curiosity soon got the better of me.

In complete contrast to the trappings (incense, pictures of the guru, etc.) that pervaded Gurudeva Ji's ashram, Sarah's home and demeanor were quite down to earth. She was a middle aged woman (like my Yoga teacher, again

Jewish), who lived in a tidy Chicago suburb. There were a few crystals placed discreetly around the house, but the scene was otherwise entirely ordinary.

That is, until I lay down on her couch. A strong ray of heat emanated from Sarah's hand as she placed it above my forehead. I demanded, literally, to look up her sleeve—to satisfy myself she wasn't holding a small flashlight or other device.

In many sessions with Sarah over the next five years, her psychic gifts were manifest. On a number of occasions, she predicted specific events, or the impact certain people would be having on me. There were also phenomenological demonstrations.

For example, I once mentioned to Sarah that streetlights seemed peculiarly to be going out as I drove by. At lunch an hour later, the ceiling lamp nearest our table expired. The unruly fixture was ten or twenty feet behind Sarah, but when I called it to her attention, she didn't turn around. She merely lowered her head and closed her eyes . . . and that light came right back on!

Fascinated as I was by such displays, my agenda with Sarah wasn't psychic titillation but spiritual counseling. I continued to assume there was more to life than earning a living, but whatever that might be, I certainly didn't feel connected to it. In the meantime, I could neither recreate nor explain away the intoxicating spiritual sensations I'd credited to Gurudeva Ji.

Sarah served as a bridge between my inspired spiritual past and my current, workaday life. Rightly or wrongly, I didn't feel I could get what I needed from traditional psychotherapy, which seemed to lack any frame of reference for my experiences as a devotee. Neither could my family help me sort things out. They were only glad I'd stopped having whatever hallucinations had attracted me to the guru in the first place.

But Sarah could and did reassure me that the events described above were real (if, perhaps, overrated). She made it clear at the outset that she herself had little use for gurus—and no interest in becoming one to me. She charged a modest hourly fee for each session. Like any good counselor, she mostly listened, giving me occasional feedback.

But where a therapist might have used my body language or choice of words to gain an understanding of my conflict, Sarah was as likely to comment on what my *aura* was doing as I recounted a particular experience. She also intuited information, sometimes with attribution to what she called "spirit guides."

Their input could be verbal, symbolic, or even psychosomatic. For example, Sarah might have an acute physical reaction to something I said—the sudden cramping of a muscle, a cough, an itch, or some other manifestation we'd both try to interpret. At a minimum, this would alert us that the symptom-triggering words warranted further exploration.

One such phrase, at the start of our work together, was "valuable but not gratifying." I had used it in describing some event that had benefited me professionally but which I'd not particularly enjoyed. All my adult life, it seemed, I'd been torn between pursuits that were remunerative/practical, on one side of the ledger, and satisfying/uplifting, on the other.

This evoked, for Sarah, two parallel sets of railroad tracks. "It's like you're running powerful but redundant engines, side by side," she commented—"an awfully inefficient way to get anywhere. Each train hauls its own cargo —your everyday stuff here, some spiritual regalia there—as though one were meat and the other, dairy."*

"But both are taking you to the same place, Adam. The tracks are *parallel*, not perpendicular."

I did feel sidetracked by those years as a devotee of Gurudeva Ji. Had I been content to remain in the ambitious frame of mind that had served me so well as a law student, I'd have stayed at the prestigious firm that recruited me right out of school. I'd probably be a partner there by now, well on my way to financial security.

On one hand, I was determined not to let my penchant for soul searching further compromise my career. Yet I longed to re-experience what I took to be the heightened consciousness of my early days as a devotee.

"Show me what that *looks* like," Sarah interjected. This took me by surprise, and in my depressed state, I doubted I could demonstrate what it was like to be "blissed out." Nevertheless, I closed my eyes and began taking the slow, deep breaths that used to catapult me into meditative oblivion. To my further surprise, I quite easily attained the sensation.

*Jewish law requires a strict separation between meat and dairy products.

"You really do go way out of your body," Sarah commented. "As for the quality or 'hue' you've been pining for, it's called 'purple.'"

"Purple?" I questioned. "What are you talking about?"

"Your aura became quite purple as you went into that meditation. There's nothing wrong with that. Purple's a nice, even a 'high' color."

"But suppose you were a painter, standing before your easel . . . with a palette full of beautiful colors—the entire rainbow. Yet the only one you chose to paint with was your favorite, purple. Don't you see how limiting this would be to you as an artist?"

"Blue, yellow, red and green will all feel *different* than purple, but they're no less self-expressive. And they'll add immensely to your finished product if you can just incorporate them."

Sarah's words didn't get me high. Nor did they resolve or even address certain psychodynamics that had caused me, all my life, to play the purple/spiritual off against my other "colors." But I'll always cherish the insight she provided that day, which truly cast my conflict in a different light.

In subsequent sessions, we continued to work on my self-limiting notion that life and its activities were either spiritual or practical. And my all-or-nothing attitude about the validity of my experiences in either realm.

"How can it be," I persisted, "that 'God' would have taken the trouble to make contact in response to my prayer, only to lead me on such a wild goose chase? I'd never have proceeded down this spiritual dead-end without those vivid experiences—a cosmic meditation here, a set of magical coincidences there . . . things that had never happened to me before. I don't want to talk myself out of the reality of my 'spiritual life.' Yet given the frustration to which it's led me, how can I *not* invalidate it?"

Sarah went silent. "I'm reluctant to repeat this," she hesitated; "you're not going to like it."

"*Out* with it, Sarah," I demanded.

"Well, what 'he' just said is, 'Even a flower . . . needs shit to grow.'"

PART TWO

RELATION

Midrash For Part Two:
The Kotzker Rebbe Rides Again*

In her sermon for *Shabbat Yitro,*** a learned, but some would say, rather "New-Age" rabbi stirred the following pot:

> How would we behave, my friends, if we were down to our last loaf of bread? Would we bring it to the daily *minyan?**** Would we hoard it for "our own"?

> What does each of us do, routinely, for the sake of our physical survival? How, in other words, do we *get* stuff? Does it come at anyone else's expense? And with whom do we share the stuff we get . . . on what terms?

> These may sound like mundane or elementary ethical questions, but I hope, in time, to convince you that they are the most profound—the most *spiritual* ones we face.

---

*Rabbi Menachem Mendl, of Kotsk, d. 1859, was famous for his sometimes ferocious honesty. A recluse toward the end of his life, the Rebbe apparently committed some heretical act (which his followers, out of respect, would never specifically identify).

**Yitro (after Moses' father-in-law, Jethro) is the Sabbath on which the Ten Commandments are read in the synagogue.

***A prayer group of ten or more.

To that end, let's begin with the familiar but enigmatic phrase from Exodus 31:17, *"Uvayom hash'vii, shavat vayinafash"*—"On the seventh day, God ceased His work and rested." Interestingly, this differs from Genesis 2:2, which says, simply, *"vayishbot bayom hash'vii,"*—"He *rested* on the seventh day." *"Shavat,"* in the one formula, and *"vayishbot,"* in the other, are the same verb (from which *"Shabbat,"* or "Sabbath," also derives).

But there's a second verb in the Exodus version, *"vayinafash,"* which comes from the root *"nefesh,"* or "soul." We could say that in His fathomless, Divine Soul, God felt satisfied, or fulfilled by what He had wrought. In that vein, Nachmanides* even suggests that those who observe the Sabbath are granted an *extra* soul for the day.

But I'll tell you what I think *"vayinafash"* really means here. I think the seventh day is when we got *our* soul—not some extra one, but the one that makes us who we are. From this point of view, God didn't just rest from His labors on *Shabbat;* He didn't just "feel complete." He passed the creative torch over *to us!* Or, perhaps more accurately, we picked it up and *ran* with it.

I'm not suggesting God bowed out of the creative process altogether. As we say in our morning prayer, *"Uv'tuvo m'chadeysh b'chol yom tamid maaseh b'reyshit"*—"In His goodness, He renews daily the work of creation." And we say, *"shehecheyanu v'ki-*

*Rabbi Moshe ben Nachman, 1194-1270.

manu"—"He fashions and *sustains* us" (in all our physical parameters).

But I'm going to ask you, now, *chevre* [friends], to think of this physical world as just a backdrop for a different kind of creativity. Picture the whole magnificent package—the heavens above and the earth below, the world and all that dwell therein—as a staging ground, a *tabula rasa,* for the next, *non-physical* round of creation. In which the most generative element, the *stem cell* for all our future growth, is . . . this may surprise you . . . our individual *self-interest!* The very thing we bit into (or bit off) when Adam and Eve ate from the Tree of Knowledge.

Stay with me here, *chevre;* I know this is getting a bit deep. In the cosmology I'm asking you to entertain, Adam and Eve turn God's orderly physical creation into their own *"tohu vavohu"*—their own "primordial soup." A place of material shortage and economic need. From which raw material *we* must now renew daily the work of *relational* creation!

What I'm suggesting is that in the Garden, we were like all the other animals—the top dogs, perhaps. Only *outside* Eden's safe and comfortable confines, at the synapse between the physical/sensational and the interpersonal/relational, could human life, as we know it, begin.

In this sense, our "original sin" had little to do with the Tree of Knowledge. It was Adam and Eve's thrust for relation—the *second* big bang of creation—that did not sit well in Heaven.

"SO YOU WANT A RELATIONSHIP," boomed the Lord of Genesis to Eve. "Well, suffer the pain of childbirth—then you'll have something to *relate* to your husband (and all those little ones) about! And you, Adam, will have to clothe and feed them. You may rue the day Eve convinced you there was more to life than frequent, unprotected sex!"

"You say you ate of the forbidden fruit in order to be like *God?* The truth is, you want to *surpass* God. I, the Lord, am ONE. Now, good luck to *both* of you."

If this sounds disrespectful, *chevre,* I don't mean to be. The God I worship is the Master of all—the physical/sensational *and* what I'm calling the relational/interpersonal. But in all honesty, this biblical God seems . . . I must speak my truth, here . . . small-minded, even vindictive. I frankly find it hard to capitalize his g! For my own sanity at such awkward moments, I've taken to calling him . . . I hope you can handle this, *chevre* . . . "little god."

But as we see in today's portion, it wasn't long before little god repented of his solitude, choosing the Children of Israel with whom to experience relationship *for himself.* Now here, in *Yitro*—while his higher Self is blessing us with the gift of the Ten Commandments—little god is attaching to them a congenital string:

In the event of disobedience, he vows to visit the iniquity of the parents upon the children. And by that pronouncement, *chevre,* psychology was born.

Psychology is the impact of our ensuing misbehavior unto the third and fourth generations. We thus become the instruments of little god's impassioned discipline, inflicting collective punishment on each other. And to our great shame . . . and *this,* my friends (not our reproductive organs), was the source of that shame . . . on our own offspring.

The therapists call this "displacement." Mom and Dad's original sins are first "displaced" onto our significant others, with whom we continue to act out what are, in reality, generational conflicts. Soon enough, our children become props in the emotional drama, thereby acquiring their grievances against us.

It took one for sensation, two for relation; and three or four such stiff-necked generations to enmesh ourselves in little god's neurotic conundrum. Now, added to the problem of how to get things and what to share with whom, we must differentiate between fallout from our current getting, sharing and refusing to share and conflicts that are old (or someone else's).

My friends, only by unraveling this great psychospiritual puzzle can we hope to free ourselves and our progeny from a covenant that's in need of renegotiating. For we've been backpedaling since the day Adam and Eve called sensation into the service of latent relation. Our emotional exile is a vestige of little god's primordial hurt feelings. We must help him (and ourselves) get *over* it.

Shabbat shalom.

4

Dor Vador
(Generation to Generation)

The significance of the following incident will become apparent as the story of my marriage unfolds. It occurred before I'd met my wife-to-be, or even had a serious romantic relationship.

I was taking a beginning acting course as part of my general, liberal arts requirements at Purdue. At that stage of my life, I eschewed all emotional self-expression, regarding "feelings" as excuses weak people made for not having their lives together (like mine was). Consistent with that attitude, I conceived of actors as people who recited dialogue, throwing in a hand gesture here and a facial expression there, as necessary to make the scene convincing.

Since I didn't *believe* in feelings, I certainly couldn't see any value in trying to "identify emotionally" (whatever that might mean) with any character I might be asked to play. I came into this class expecting simply to memorize and then "enact" (with all appropriate panache) whatever script might be handed me.

Instead, our liberal airhead of an instructor was into improvisation. He asked me to "dig deep" and come up with "my own material."

While I waited outside the room, my classmates cooked up a scene to which I would have to respond spontaneously. All I was told by way of preparation was that I was returning home from work to my wife of several years.

I walked in, on cue, to discover "my wife" in bed with another man. I surveyed the situation momentarily . . . then simply refused to play my assigned part.

It's not that I was taken aback in any moralistic sense by the scene that confronted me. If I'd had a script, I certainly could have read the husband's lines and mustered some theatrical affect. But I lacked all capacity to identify with his predicament and *react* to it. Being so out of touch with my own feelings, I was, in the absence of canned dialogue, at a literal loss for words.

My stunted emotional condition was matched (or compensated for) by the smug assumption that my own carefully scripted life would never subject me to any such experience. No one I married would be capable of such a betrayal. How, then, could I be expected to identify with this pathetic character?

Three decades later, it's clear that my defensive armor simply didn't permit the kind of spontaneity the acting instructor was asking of me. I was one of the last to realize that my entire personality at the time was pre-scripted dialogue.

I have a younger brother, Earl, who seems as cut off from his feelings today as I was at the time of my acting debut. It was in a conversation with him, not too many years ago, that the root of our emotional problem came into bold relief. Thinking myself to have matured substantially by that time, I presumed to offer my brother some feedback on his lagging psychological development. "I can't seem to make contact with you," I goaded. "It's like you're 'not home,' emotionally."

Earl deflected the provocation briefly, then retaliated with the following jab of his own: "Don't expect me to feel one way or the other *about you*. I can't give you what you want. It's nothing personal; I just do not *feel*."

I was taken aback by the incisiveness with which my brother thus cut to the chase, both of our interaction and of his psychological predicament. I asked if he'd always been this way, or could he recall ever having had a "feeling?"

Earl answered with hardly a moment's hesitation: "I was about seven. Dad was ranting at Mother, and I was standing there, crying. 'Why is Daddy mad?' I asked. 'It's not Daddy,' she answered, 'it's the alcohol.'"

Earl's immediate retrieval of this incident in response to my query spoke volumes to me. We'd grown up with an alcoholic father and a passive-aggressive mother. Gerald would verbally abuse Abby each night, while she made herself morally superior and thus "impervious" to the insults. The effect of her pronouncement, "It's not Daddy, it's the alcohol," was to anesthetize my brother, emotionally, by depersonalizing the experience. With one fell swoop, she severed emotional effect from behavioral cause.

This may be how all psychological defenses begin. We try to protect those we love by distracting them from the source of their discomfort. But when Earl asked, "Why is Daddy mad," Daddy truly was angry. Earl found this upsetting, but he was at least in touch with his own resulting turmoil.

From that day forward, however, he stopped allowing his interactions to register emotionally. Psychology calls this "denial." My father had hurt Earl's feelings; my mother had relieved him of them.

Denying or depersonalizing our pain may seem to make sense when, as in the case of seven-year-old Earl, there's really nothing we can do about the external circumstances that are causing it. The problem is, the habit of denial robs us of the ability to enjoy improved relational conditions when they finally arrive. Subconsciously, we continue to experience life as though still confronted with whatever first put our feelings on hold.*

In summary, my siblings and I were taught to depersonalize the most personal of our interactions. Since it made no sense to be angry at an inanimate bottle of alcohol, Mother's implicit advice was to disregard the emotional upheaval we were experiencing. To "tune out" the most dramatic events of our interpersonal lives.

Gerald, in turn, reinforced our denial by waking up stone sober each morning, as though nothing untoward had occurred the night before. This was our positive male role model—strong and handsome; competent and *un*emotional.

Emotion thus came to be equated, in our minds, with the destructive tirades "the alcohol" inflicted on us each evening. The choice seemed either to blame the alcohol (like Mother) or *become* the alcohol (like Father).

*And to rationalize this muted (but now inexplicable) discomfort, we make sure to keep a supply of current-time adversity on hand. Psychology calls this the "repetition compulsion."

My way of dealing with my dad's verbal attacks was different from my brother's, however. I was more combative, mouthing off as much as I dared, until forced to retreat from the room or the house. I further distracted myself from this adverse home life by becoming an overachiever. I threw myself into the B'nai B'rith Youth Organization, eventually rising to the presidency of a four-state district. Between my organizational life, schoolwork, choir performances and synagogue activities, I kept myself a very busy and well-adjusted looking young man.

By age 16, I was a Goldwater Republican. I went on to read Ayn Rand's *Atlas Shrugged,* with its ideologically impassioned but unemotional heroes. And by the time I reached that acting class at Purdue, I was acting a lot like Michael J. Fox's smug character, Alex P. Keaton (in the television series *Family Ties*).

But a funny thing happened to me on the way to the Nixon White House. I met Diane.

She was the antithesis of the personality I've just described: soft, warm and demonstratively affectionate. She had an innate capacity to make people feel at ease and draw them out. Her mission in life was to lighten me up, and her agenda threatened my Republicanism and my machismo.

I'll have more to say about Diane's dynamics later, but before leaving the story of my individual emotional development, I want to fast-forward to my previously described life as a devotee. How could the carefully scripted character in the current chapter have been drawn, only a few years later, to the seemingly intimate and entirely extemporaneous spirituality of my cousin Jeff and his fellow devotees? How did I myself find the capacity, on the very heels of my acting class fiasco, to speak so movingly and *improvisationally* about Gurudeva Ji?

What I've come to understand is that these personae, the worldly, ambitious Adam and the spiritual, introspective one, were two sides of the same unemotional coin. Like my father, I could transform myself from an extroverted but tightly controlled presentation into a state of *spiritual* intoxication. But in psychological reality, these two stances were more similar than disparate. What they had in common was their total detachment from any relational context or emotional self-expression.

What I needed to learn was how to paint the picture of my life using not just the purple color of passive spirituality (or whatever color my Michael J. Fox persona epitomized). To show my *true* colors—even as they might change from situation to situation. To correct the inconsistency between my outward appearance and what I wasn't allowing myself to feel. To communicate with emotional content, not just audience pleasing theatrics.

In short, to reengage my interpersonal apparatus. As a complement to whatever intellectual and spiritual acumen I'd begun to develop.

5

Tanya and Sherman

By the early '80s, the channelers had largely supplanted the gurus at the vanguard of the New-Age. Their books were on the best seller lists, and Tanya, among others, was criss-crossing the country.

When she came through Chicago, I considered attending one of her public demonstrations. I ran the idea by Sarah, whose own channeled input was, "Adam might find this of interest."

I should say a word about Sarah's type of channeling and how it differed from what I was about to experience. Indeed, Tanya's own alter ego, "Mr. Dillon," once explained it this way:

> This is called "dead trance," where Tanya leaves her body, and I come through. Then there's the trance where the person feels the spirit and gives the message, like a psychic reading, which can be good, too.

Sarah fell into the latter category. She herself was fully present while intuiting the message. It thus remained her choice whether to pass any or all of it along. Tanya, however, claimed to be absent from her body and oblivious to what was being said by Dillon. Theirs was like a landlord-tenant relationship: The body still belonged to Tanya, but for the duration of the trance, Dillon's occupancy was exclusive.

Tanya began the program by explaining the mechanics of trance, as she understood them, and the ground rules for how we would proceed. The lights were then dimmed, and someone with a guitar began leading us in Bette Midler's "The Rose."

Tanya seated herself and closed her eyes. A moment later, her head slumped forward. We sang on, watching for the next telling twitch.

Suddenly, the head jerked back upright and the eyes popped open. The mouth smiled, more on one side than the other. And in a strong, masculine sounding voice, the words "FAITH AND FELICITY BE WITH YE!" rang out.

"Mr. Dillon" now spoke for several minutes on some general spiritual theme. I don't remember his specific topic that night, but we were utterly charmed by his presence. His personality, vocabulary and sense of humor were quite unlike Tanya's. (Indeed, as Dillon was later to point out, most people found it easier to relate to him than to Tanya.)

We were enthralled by tales of psychic wizardry at these early trance sessions. A man who'd previously asked Dillon about a problem knee now reported having awakened, that same night, in a peculiar position—up on all fours, but with the bad leg extended behind him. And from then on, the knee had given him no further trouble.

He went on to describe a dream in which he thought Dillon had communicated with him. I was seated near the front of the room that evening, up close to Tanya/Dillon. As the man related Dillon's dream-message, I could hear Dillon, under his breath (or Tanya's) *anticipating* it, word for word.

By the time Diane and I met Tanya/Dillon, our relationship had again deteriorated, to the point we were barely speaking. In fact, I hadn't mentioned the trance circle to her until the last moment and was surprised when she asked to come along.

At first, Dillon displayed an uncanny awareness of our personalities and relational gridlock. But then he asked us if we'd like to be married. Diane politely informed him we'd been married for twelve years. "I'm talking about being married 'in the spirit,'" Dillon replied. "Would you like to be married *by me?*"

Diane quickly took him up on the offer, her enthusiasm again catching me off guard. For all the distance between us, there had been no talk of divorce. But neither had I contemplated re-upping, much less for multiple lifetimes. I'll digress here to explain a tenet of Dillon's teaching that was coming into play (though at the time, we were just vaguely aware of it).

He taught that each soul has an "eternal soulmate"—a preordained spouse. A match literally made in heaven. Such soulmates have a synergistic effect on each other's individual (spiritual) growth. The relational whole is greater than the sum of its parts.

Diane and I were eventually converted to this vision of marriage, which became the central theme of our apprenticeships with Tanya/Dillon (and Tanya's own husband,

Sherman). If Gurudeva Ji was supposed to have shown me how to speak to God, they would teach the two of us how to approach Him as a relationship.

And how to speak to each other. With guest appearances by Dillon, Tanya and Sherman offered a three-day seminar, billed as a life-changing event for the couple. It was, for the relationship, what *shaktiput* (initiation) was for the individual spiritual seeker.

This was quite different from the spiritual counseling I'd experienced with Sarah. She didn't offer conjoint sessions, nor was she focused on relational issues as such. But when I raised the eternal soulmate concept during my transition from her tutelage to Tanya and Sherman's, she took exception to it.

Sarah went so far as to suggest that from a psychospiritual point of view, Diane and I were, if anything, a *mismatch*. In all events, she rejected the idea of a preordained, "Mr. or Ms. Right" for each person and for all time.

But Tanya and Sherman lumped relationships into two categories: "eternal" and "karmatic." "Karmatic" meant the pair was together to resolve conflicts left over from a prior lifetime. This was important work, but once the karma was addressed, the relationship had no further *raison d'etre*.

Eternal soulmates might have their own conjugal karma to clean up. But they would then blossom as a couple—lifting each other, in the process, to their highest individual potentials.

I should mention that Tanya and Sherman were willing to assume that any couple who came to them *were* eternal soulmates. What this meant, as a practical matter, was that they'd be held to the high standard of marital accountability (and collective scrutiny) I'll be describing below. If this proved too difficult for either spouse, i.e., if the rigors of living life in such an intensely communicative fashion ended up driving the couple apart rather than bringing them closer together, that would show that the relationship was merely karmatic.

Such couples could go on creating still more karma for each other. Or they could work diligently to resolve past and present grievances . . . and move on to find with whom they everlastingly belonged.

As noted above, my experience of the preceding twelve years cast immediate doubt on any assumption Diane and I were meant to be together "for all time." So (like any prudent lawyer attending his first trance circle), I demanded Dillon's personal assurance that we were, indeed, "eternal soulmates." Only then did I allow him to place his blessing on the relationship.

I don't remember anything out of the ordinary taking place at our nuptials the next day (except that they were being performed by a dead man, speaking through a woman's body). We repeated our vows, exchanged new rings and I kissed the bride.

In addition to such matchmaking services, Dillon offered us individual guidance. With respect to my singing, for instance, he told me the problem was that my "throat *chakra*"* was closed. I asked if he could help me get it *open,* to which he replied:

---

*Yogananda described the *chakras* as "occult cerebrospinal centers," the awakening of which "is the sacred goal of the yogi."

Well, one way is to tell the truth all the time and live your life in integrity. That, my son, allows for all the gifts of the spirit, which music is, to open up.

But the greatest gift I can give you, Adam, is my sense of humor! To be able to *laugh* as you sing is joyful in God, is it not? So, what you have to do is, come, tomorrow, with a song to sing *for me!*

Dillon then asked if we had any instruments, and someone offered up a bass fiddle they'd dubbed "Barbara." Now *Dillon* began to sing:

> Big Brown *Babs,* she does it well!
> *She'll* make Adam sing cuz he'll
> *go to hell* if he
> doesn't sing!

> A-dam . . . A-*dumb!*
> *You* think you're in *court,*
> when you *really* need to be
> drinkin' *up the port!*

This cracked everyone up but me. "I really *do* want to sing," I persisted, as if the trick was just getting through to Dillon how badly I wanted it. "I've worked at this so many years, trying all the while to maintain some kind of spiritual perspective."

"Oh Gaaaaahhhddd . . . ," Dillon moaned. "*Will* Adam be 'spiritual' *in court?* Tune in next week!"

Thus did he humor us through our attachments and obsessions.

I want to turn, however, to what Tanya and Sherman, in their own flesh and blood, had to offer. They'd come to town every several months to conduct what amounted to group therapy sessions, focused largely on our marital relationships. On the weekends in between these formal sessions, the Chicago group would socialize and "process"* together. Although we were all obviously interested in psychic phenomena and spiritual growth, we also spent time just getting to know one another.

The trance itself gradually became less the focus of our weekend soirees, even when Tanya and Sherman were with us. I began to appreciate Sherman's own intuitive gift, looking more and more to him as a kind of spiritual big brother. And there was always a sense of the psychic present, to guide and inspire any of us as we processed our personal issues and relational conflicts.

During one such session, for example, I'd been unable to get in touch with anything remotely resembling a feeling (as distinguished from a thought) about what was bothering me. I'd been sitting for some time against a wall, beneath a window. As my frustration mounted, Tanya's ten-year-old daughter, who was playing outside, suddenly slammed the window shut behind me. The physical jolt threw me into an immediate rage.

Tanya reined me in, stating: "My daughter is very psychic. Please don't aim you're anger at her." I took this to mean the girl had somehow been guided to slam that window, thus provoking me into contact with the rage I'd been trying all morning to get in touch with. It was as if an emotional boil had been lanced.

---

* "Processing" means stepping back from the task or subject at hand to deal with underlying, interpersonal issues.

But within moments, the anger shifted to an overwhelming sadness. "It's my *father,"* I blurted out, not knowing why I was saying that. This led to a prolonged account of my relationship with my dad, which, though not at all the focus of my earlier process, was now imbued with an emotional substance my previous sharing had entirely lacked.

It's not that I remembered any new facts about our relationship. It's just that my emotions were now reuniting with their subject matter. I was finally able to access the pain we'd all known was "in there," but which I'd been unable, until that moment, to *feel.* (Such a reunion of thought and feeling, I've since come to believe, is the beginning of all emotional healing.)

For about a year, we continued our weekly get-togethers with the members of this marital support group (and with Tanya and Sherman on about a bimonthly basis). I also continued to visit, intermittently, with Sarah. In one of those sessions, I told her we were about to spend three days alone with Tanya and Sherman, taking their "Eternal Marital Relationship Seminar."

On hearing this, Sarah furrowed her brow and expressed some concern over what she foresaw for me at this event. "Take plenty of vitamin C," she encouraged, "and try to get a lot of rest; it's not going to be easy work."

During that same session, Sarah took me through a hypnotic, "past-life regression." I saw myself as a rabbi, married to Diane. Our relationship, as in the present, was a cold one. Diane had done something—I couldn't get the specifics, but it was in the nature of a religious or moral transgression. I had convened a rabbinic court to address the matter, having made a firm if painful decision that my wife must be treated no differently than anyone else in the administration of religious law.

Diane never forgave what she considered my excessive show of principle. For the rest of that lifetime together, she was obedient but distant. Just as I'd insisted on the letter of the law, so she now performed her wifely duties to the letter, but entirely without spirit.

At this point, Sarah asked me to envision our last interaction in that lifetime. I saw myself at Diane's deathbed. I was terribly repentant for the choice I had made. "If only I could go back and do it differently," I lamented, "I'd make *her* more important than any religious principle."

"Your prayer was heard," Sarah interjected. "The current life is your opportunity to make that different choice."

My experience of this session is hard to categorize—I can't say I felt either deeply hypnotized or vividly aware of the imagery in a pictorial sense. It was more like free association than watching a movie.

Yet I was having an intense *emotional* response as I described these scenes to Sarah. I felt the profound grief of the rabbi, kneeling at the bedside of his dying wife. Whether it was my life or anyone's I was visualizing, some kind of catharsis seemed to be taking place.

Sarah didn't alert me to any connection between the above and the "hard work" I was about to do with Tanya and Sherman. (Nor did I tell them anything about my session with her.) But during the first day of the marital marathon, Sherman began prodding Diane.

He asked her, gently but persistently, if there was something she wanted to get off her chest. Eventually, she confirmed his intuition . . . that she'd been having an affair.

I was devastated by this revelation. We spent the next several days filling in every bitter detail—and every other secret my wife had kept from me (or I from her). As Sarah had predicted, this was one of the most stressful emotional experiences of my life.

But through the tumultuous days and weeks that followed, I took consolation in the session with Sarah that had preceded Diane's disclosure. The Rabbi's regret—and Sarah's suggestion I behave differently this time around—held out a silver lining: the possibility that real growth might result from this catastrophe, depending on how I handled it.

Diane was remorseful and begged my forgiveness. As bad as things were, there was at least a framework in place, under Tanya and Sherman's auspices, for our eventual reconciliation.

Indeed, if they were right about the eternal soulmate concept, perhaps—just perhaps—the wreckage of our marriage could be hauled away and the foundation laid for a different kind of relationship. One in which I might find both the spiritual and the interpersonal substance I'd long been craving.

6

Picking Up the Pieces

The total breakdown of my marriage that came to light in the session with Tanya and Sherman would have forced me to reassess my life and goals even if soul-searching hadn't already become, for me, an avocation. By now, we'd been to mainstream, Ph.D. and M.S.W.-type marriage counselors, and Diane had been in treatment with two different psychoanalysts. Nevertheless, and despite the shambles we'd made of our marriage, neither one of us seemed ready to call it a marital day.

Tanya and Sherman, meanwhile, were assuring us that the "healing" of our relationship had already begun. If we wanted to accelerate the process, they and several other couples were forming what amounted to a live-in support group for dysfunctional families. In, of all places, a town called Normal, Illinois.

They described it as a community in which, under Mr. Dillon's ultimate authority, the participants would pursue their individual spiritual development while reconstituting their marriages and family lives. It seemed a unique opportunity to turn our adversity to advantage. With one stroke, we could make a clean physical break from our sordid past and begin a new spiritual adventure.

When Sarah answered the door on my next visit, her greeting was, "Going somewhere? Come in and tell me about it." In spite of some misgivings about Tanya and Sherman, she was respectful of Tanya's psychic gift and never questioned the reality of Mr. Dillon. She also intimated we'd gain much from this experience in the wilds of Central Illinois.

For our families and friends, we tried to make the transition as respectable looking as possible. There were plenty of good reasons to be moving out of Chicago in the spring of 1983. I told my academic colleagues it was time for me to return to private practice, and that I preferred to do so in a smaller-town environment. There was so much crime and traffic in the city. And with the equity we'd accrued in our tiny, three-bedroom house, we'd be able to afford a veritable palace in Normal.

All these things, of course, were true but beside the point.

Like us, the other couples moving to Tanya and Sherman's community were struggling, to one degree or another, to hold their marriages together. About half (including Sherman) were Jewish. There was another lawyer, another psychiatric social worker, a psychology professor, a medical school professor and, a bit later, a dentist. Along with our collective emotional baggage, we shared an egalitarian vision of communal living and psychological self-help.

We purchased five large homes, all on the same block, in a nice residential neighborhood. We developed a home-schooling program for the children. The idea was to create a self-contained community, in which our kids would be surrounded by a nurturing, extended family. We'd all feel welcome in any of the five households. And we'd be knowledgeable of and engaged in each other's personal and familial processes.

To that end, but also for economic reasons, we lived two to three families per house. For while some of us had arrived with money in the bank, the group included waiters, delivery-people, construction workers . . . and lots of kids. As a result, our mission to save our marriages came also to entail forging community, under these emotionally dire but adventuresome circumstances, across social and economic lines. Just as husbands and wives were recommitting to each other as eternal soulmates, our families were undertaking to share all aspects of the communal burden—social, psychological, spiritual and economic.

Neither Diane nor I had ever been involved in anything so radical. But we were doing this together. We were once again on the same team. And we believed we were finally turning our dysfunctional relationship into something truly noble.

As I recall these early, halcyon days in the community, I'm still struck by our bold idealism. Here we were, eventually forty or so adults, many of us professionally if not interpersonally accomplished, committing ourselves and our resources to a common vision of marital and communal life we were learning and inventing as we went along.

We were going to help each other uproot all vestiges of selfishness, pride, deceitfulness and self-suppression. We'd work diligently, within each relationship and household, to handle every interpersonal conflict and every practical challenge of daily living at the inspired level we'd experienced during our weekend sessions with Tanya and Sherman.

And for the first year or so—while we were able to live off our savings—the experience was truly exhilarating.

7

Energy

I've just returned from a lecture by Rabbi and author Joseph Telushkin, who previewed his new book, *Words That Hurt; Words That Heal*. Telushkin's topic was "the ethics, not the psychology" of human communication. He calls for the creation of a national day on which everyone will refrain from uttering even a single harsh or hurtful word.

As I'll attempt to explain below, the Rabbi's focus on our verbal output (rather than the more elusive psychology and spirit of the interaction) is just the opposite of what we were shooting for in the community. We believed the integrity of our communication, certainly in the husband and wife context, was a function of the emotional authenticity (not the words *per se*) with which we expressed ourselves. This made the internal conflicts and relational issues animating the hurtful speech more germane than the words themselves.

While my view of this has moderated in the intervening years, I still believe great and small harm is regularly inflicted by "appropriate" words, which, like undetectable carbon monoxide, do their damage via the nonverbal energy that escorts them. Unless and until the underlying hostility is addressed, it continues to injure our loved ones and ourselves, whether we soften the verbal blows or censor them entirely. The challenge, in short, is to manage not the words but the much subtler communicative essence, which, though expressed through our words, exerts a destructive (or beneficent) influence in and of itself.

As though anticipating the above, the Rabbi reminded his audience that our first duty is to behave decently, however we may be feeling on the inside. Better to feed the hungry, even with resentment, than to hold out, at their expense, for some psychospiritual epiphany. The fundamental precept of *tzedaka* (righteousness) commands us to relieve what suffering we can, and strive for a more loving spirit *(kavana)* as we go along.

Judaism thus assigns a higher value to *tikun olam* ("repair of the world") than to personal salvation. One's speech, Telushkin argues, is no less subject to this behavioral mandate. So until we can rise above our hurtful sentiments, we should find the self-control to muzzle them . . . at least for one day out of the year.

Of course, true *tzaddikim* (righteous ones) have managed to combine the letter *with* the spirit of the law. These great souls are exalted in Jewish literature and storytelling. In Buber's *Tales of the Chasidim,* he recounts a disciple of one such *tzaddik* proclaiming, "I didn't go to the [Master] in order to hear Torah from him but to see how he unlaces his felt shoes and laces them up again." This reminds me of a statement by Ralph Waldo Emerson: "I and mine do not teach by argument, but by our *presence."*

In the psychological world, there's a similar debate between the behaviorists, on one side, and the psychoanalysts, on the other. The former say, "Enough plumbing of the subconscious depths; let's clean up this patient's act!" The latter say, "Give us a few more years of treatment and we'll surely get to the root of the problem. We can then effect a cure, instead of just masking the symptoms."

It wasn't 'til I arrived at Tanya and Sherman's community that I glimpsed the possibility of integrating, in a single framework, the behavioral aspect (words and deeds) with the psychospiritual processes from which our conduct emanates. That would address a concern Diane had raised at the beginning of my spiritual search: that "spirituality" was no substitute for basic psychological (behavioral) health. But going well beyond Telushkin's prescription, our goal was to become conscious of (and thereby take responsibility for) not just our choice of words but our unspoken attitudes and agendas.

It was on this level that Tanya and Sherman perceived the real spiritual and communicative challenges to lie. They had a remarkable gift for seeing the energetic forest through the behavioral trees. To the less perceptive, this sometimes made their own behavior seem inappropriate or disproportionate.

For example, on a visit to Normal before we'd decided to move there, we walked in on a heated argument between Tanya and another member of the group. Tanya became self-conscious—conflicted over whether to sweep the altercation under the rug out of deference to the social expectations of the out-of-town guests. (She was well aware that to us, her remonstrations looked unseemly, if not hysterical.)

But Tanya's vehemence reflected her and the community's commitment to "call the energy," i.e., not to sit on unexpressed emotionality. They saw disrespect not in the forceful and direct exchange of angry words but in disingenuous chatter between people who were energetically pummeling each other. That kind of socially appropriate non-communication was as offensive to them as a torrent of cuss words was to us.

Tanya did interrupt her tirade, long enough to explain that this kind of exchange was normal for them and that we needn't be unduly concerned. I professed great "cool" about the chaos we'd intruded upon (though, of course, I was politely lying through my teeth).

When things eventually calmed down, Tanya elaborated that the community's way was to respond "cleanly" but otherwise uninhibitedly to the energy of the moment. Just as soon as that energy "shifted," it would be as though the conflict had never existed. For once the energy (not just the rhetoric) had truly changed, there would literally be no grudge left to hold.

As I acclimated myself to this no-holds-barred way of interacting, I found it much more alive and honest than what passes for communication in the more polite company to which we were accustomed. I also came to agree with Tanya that the energy of conflict truly does dissipate just as soon as it's been fully and cleanly addressed—and not a moment before. The devil, of course, is in the details. But the development of our attunement to energy, sufficiently to recognize when it was "off" (in conflict) and when it had shifted (resolution), would be a large part of our work over the next three years in Normal.

I'm sure many psychically gifted people can actually "see" this energy shift, perhaps as a change in the person's aura. Any good therapist uses his own intuitive faculties to recognize when a moment of emotional reality breaks through the chatter of ordinary, defensive banter; when the defenses have been sufficiently penetrated to allow both the consciousness and the behavior to truly change. Whether we speak in psychological or psychic terms, the process is the same. The person finally "gets" (realizes) that small piece of his life's puzzle, and the air is somehow, almost miraculously, cleared.

This differentiation between words and their underlying energy did not come easy to me, however. Indeed, I dismissed it, at first, as so much New-Age psychobabble. Not surprisingly, this created tension between me and the group. They accused me of concealing my own hostility behind lawyer-like words and convincing arguments. And for an excruciating time, I really had no clue what these people were talking about.

An early incident will illustrate just how out of touch I was. A few days after moving to Normal, I found myself in a room with Sherman and two of the men, engaged in some rather lively if egotistical banter about the great spiritual things we were going to do together. I made some comment I no longer recall that evoked from Sherman a slightly teasing but affectionate response: "Oh, am I such a heavy *burden* to you?"

Without the slightest consciousness of any hostility toward Sherman, I replied: "You're not a heavy burden; you're just *fat.*"

Sherman stood up and walked out of the room. A hush fell over the three of us who remained, but didn't last long. Tanya came flying in, the quick upshot of which was, I was ordered to leave the house!

I left, shaken, apologetic and profoundly confused. An emissary soon came to inform me that I was unwelcome in Sherman's household until my energy had shifted. In the meantime, I was to communicate with him and Tanya only through third parties.

I'll not address here the disproportionality of this response to my teasing quip (or the kind of communal power structure it revealed). What I want to focus on, for the present, is the reality of the energetic body blow I had, in fact, delivered to Sherman. And what he and Tanya had to teach me about energy.

I was told the offense was particularly heinous because it came as such a sneak attack, at a time we appeared to be relaxing and enjoying each other's company. For days, I protested my motivational innocence. Unfortunately, these people only viewed "I'm sorry *if* what I said hurt you" as rubbing salt in Sherman's wound. The energy remained to be dealt with until I not only admitted but "got" the intentionality (even if unconscious)* of my hurtful words.

---

*However paradoxical, the realization that our behavior is no less intentional when it *is* unconscious was a personal breakthrough for which I'll always be indebted to Tanya and Sherman.

How often do we experience well-meaning apologies that fail to inspire any confidence the offending behavior won't soon be repeated? This isn't necessarily because the apology is insincere. It's because the energy, as distinguished from the behavior, hasn't been identified, much less corrected. Thus, until I could *feel* my hostility toward Sherman, any regret I might express could only be for the adverse consequence *I* had suffered as a result. (Meanwhile, the energy would lie in wait for another opportunity to ambush him . . . or someone else.)

Now even as thick as I was in the spring of 1983, I could not for long deny that my sarcastic remark about Sherman's weight was tactless. After some soul searching, I "got" that it was a tad provocative. But the entire fabric of my self-image balked at any notion of actual malice. (Had my mother been there, *she'd* have spoken up for me: "Oh, Sherman, you're making a mountain out of a molehill. You're too sensitive!")

But something Sherman had said, before walking out of the room, stayed with me. Giving no hint of the axe that was about to fall, he'd muttered something about a "feminine energy." Then, standing and with more conviction, he declared: *"That* was a woman!*"* Which utterance somehow evoked for me not my mother's but my *sister's* inflection, each time I replayed the tape of what had just slipped out of me.

A psychologist, looking back with me on this incident, might have probed his way to the association between my behavior on this occasion and my sister. The sudden verbal jab was her trademark in nightly skirmishes with "the alcohol." But Sherman's insight was spontaneous, not psychological. He didn't deduce my sister's influence; he *felt* it.

Of course, it was my energy (not my sister's) that assaulted him. But the linkage to her brought me around, in time, to the more pertinent question: What was *I* now lashing out against?

If all this seems too complicated, paranormal or far-fetched, we could just say I'd learned a style of fighting from my sister that I'd unleashed on Sherman, for reasons I did not yet understand. We all borrow in this way from our siblings and parents to perpetuate our distinctive family brands of what Rabbi Telushkin calls "hurtful speech." But to the extent I might attempt to pass the responsibility off to my sister or mother, they (or their therapists) could just as easily refer me further up the ancestral chain.

Every such familial legacy awaits a generation with the fortitude to say, "Enough is enough. The neurotic buck stops here. I (and my children) shall be free of this."*

I do believe my personal growth, and my children's, was thus accelerated because Tanya and Sherman did for me what no proper therapist would have agreed to do. They subjected themselves, in the relatively unprotected framework of this "spiritual community," to the unfiltered onslaught of my displacement (along with everyone else's).

---

*This should not be confused with the defiant energy psychology calls a "reaction formation" (where we make a point of doing just the opposite of what our parent(s) would have done or wanted). That behavioral strategy only reinforces the emotional legacy we think we're rejecting.

Experienced therapists know their patients' transference* can and will exploit any weakness in their professional armor. That's another reason they don't invite the patient home for tea (much less move him into the spare bedroom, as Tanya and Sherman were doing). They don't share their own hopes, fears and frustrations, lest the patient find a way to use that information against them (or to undermine the treatment).

Tanya eventually explained that just moments before my quip about Sherman's weight, he'd confided to her his increasing self-consciousness *on that very score*. Now Sherman wasn't all that obese, and it hadn't entered my conscious mind that he was sensitive about his weight. But that doesn't mean I didn't intuit his sensitivity.

Sherman and I were thus equally psychic: I, by knowing where he was vulnerable; he, by sensing my cheap shot had something to do with how the women in my life had influenced me. I doubt any therapist could have gotten the ball rolling more quickly.

In a nutshell, the concept of energy, as taught by Tanya and Sherman, meant we owed a duty—at least to those we claimed to love—to become more fully *conscious*. To take responsibility not just for our words and behavior but for the effect our very presence is having on those around us.

Based on this high standard, the community served as an extension of the eternal soulmate relationship. Indeed, we began to speak less of "community" and more of "spiritual

*The patient/client's tendency to displace his unresolved parental conflicts onto the therapist.

family." The idea, or ideal, was to extend the same high level of responsibility in our spoken and unspoken communication outward—from the nuclear family to the larger, spiritual family. And, eventually, to the stranger on the street.

That, we felt, would be the beginning of real *tikun olam.*

8

Spiritual Community

What roles, then, were we playing for each other in this unusual psychospiritual enclave? We weren't "friends," in the normal sense of that word. There was a definite hierarchy, with Mr. Dillon presumably at the top, and Tanya and Sherman taking care of the day-to-day administration of the collective energy. There were also designated "heads of household," who were the initial arbiters of what was going on among the residents of each house.

The organizational structure and spiritual aliveness reminded me, somehow, of the Children of Israel, on their departure from Egypt. We believed we'd left the bondage of our moribund relationships and psychic ignorance in Chicago, Denver, Philadelphia or wherever we'd come from. We looked to Tanya and Sherman to guide us through the uncharted relational wilderness. And we counted on an unseen, higher authority to intervene, whenever we might lose our collective, intuitive way.

As suggested above, the commitment to the eternal soulmate was the covenant upon which the social and philosophical structure of the community rested. The marital relationship was seen as both the context and the catalyst for the psychospiritual growth of the individual (and of the group as a whole). We continued to draw inspiration from Tanya's weekly trance, but it was in the small and large conflicts and energy shifts to which the grist of daily living subjected us that we waited on the Lord.

Our lives were thus filled with myriad small moments of interpersonal truth. Our psychospiritual classroom was the kitchen, the work place, the bedroom—wherever we found ourselves. We made no distinction between neurotic, relational and spiritual issues, believing any of these, if examined with courage and determination, would lead us to the Truth. We likewise assumed that our familial and communal conflicts, if handled with integrity, would bring to light and help resolve our most deep-seated individual pathologies.

9

The Eternal Soulmate Relationship: "It Guards Your Breath As It Cleans Your Teeth"

Early in our marriage, we knew a couple who could have been Mr. and Mrs. Jack Sprat. He was thin as a rail, and she was grossly obese. She eventually underwent a surgical procedure to remove part of her small intestine. The purpose of the operation was to allow food to pass more quickly through her system, which would somehow cause her to lose weight.

The operation was a success, but the relationship died. She dropped over 100 pounds; then he dropped her!

It seems self-evident that any significant change in the individual is going to impact the relationship. Is it not incongruous, therefore, for marriage counseling and individual treatment to be administered as separate disciplines? The therapist treats the individual, without input from the absent but no less impacted spouse; while the marriage counselor addresses the couple's communication, but with scant attention to root psychological issues.

We were thus enthused about combining the work of the therapist and the marriage counselor in a single venue. We believed if we were to make real and lasting progress as a couple, it would be necessary to identify and address the individual neuroses that were driving the relationship. At the same time, we felt that our individual issues were best accessed through the relationship, since that's where they most pervasively presented. Finally, we'd accepted the theory that the marital relationship (with the eternal soulmate gloss added) provided not only the arena but the spiritual catalyst through which the individuals would achieve their emotional healing.

Healing the Relationship: The Medium Is the Message

What is the goal of psychotherapy? Unlike other forms of education, its highly personal curriculum aims specifically at self-knowledge. Nor is it merely an intellectual study. Our increasing self-awareness marks our progress toward emotional and spiritual maturity.

But just as our psychospiritual deficiencies reveal themselves in our behavior, shouldn't individual growth likewise manifest, practically, in improved behavior and relationships? For what good is self-awareness if it doesn't help our relationships work better?

I'm reminded here of a conversation some twenty years ago with a med student friend, who was planning to become a psychiatrist. This young man had a surprisingly cynical attitude about his future career, shaped, in part, by his own therapeutic experience. He bluntly told me that for him, therapy "had not worked."

"What it achieved," he declared, "was the identification of my emotional issues, but without any real impact on them or their relational consequences." His devastatingly negative conclusion was that we neither feel nor behave better after therapy; we simply earn the dubious privilege of knowing just what we're *doing* to our loved ones and ourselves!

Under the eternal soulmate rubric, by contrast, our vision of emotional health was entirely functional. The relationship served as our psychological proving ground.

But what does "work better" *mean* in the marital context? Many couples are content not to rock the boat—to maintain the emotional homeostasis that attracted them to each other in the first place. And homing in on the individual energies fueling our conflicts tended, if anything, to *de*stabilize the relationships as presently constituted.

But our idea of improved communication wasn't the avoidance of overt conflict at the cost of keeping it covert. In that sense, we saw marital friction as the coin of the therapeutic realm—not to be short-changed into tidy but less evocative "I-statements."

We also knew that whoever's behavior had "started it" on this occasion, there were always reciprocal issues at play—some emotional counterpart in the spouse that made him willing to engage in the drama in the first place. This fight wouldn't be happening—this couple wouldn't *be together*—if their neuroses weren't somehow complementing one another.

We realized, in short, that what defense mechanisms are to the individual, the relational status quo is to the couple. Just as we deny our internal conflicts in a vain attempt to preserve our personal comfort, so the relationship constructs an interlocking network of defenses, looking thereto for some modicum of stability. But as the effect of denial is to cut the individual off from his feelings, so the neurotic symbiosis erodes the couple's capacity for intimacy.

We also recognized that all marital conflict is at once a symptom of and a railing against this very symbiosis. When an argument erupted, we saw it as one or the other spouse's thrust (however unconscious) for *greater* intimacy—a conjoint version of the repetition compulsion. The first step was to identify which partner was thus stirring the neurotic pot on this conflictual occasion.

Our purpose wasn't to referee the conflict or to declare one side "right" and the other "wrong." The object was to identify the person who was, in reality, calling attention to his own (individual) issue—so that it could be addressed. As we would put it, that person's energy was "up."

The Eternal Soulmate's Carrot

We believed, with all the fervor of religious acolytes, that each partner had both the capacity and the spiritual duty to help heal the other. We reasoned that the spouse could do two things the therapist could not: He could *love* the "patient"; and be there for the long haul.

I've always had trouble with Carl Rogers' claim of "unconditional positive regard" for his clients. How can this be when the very regard is metered out in 45-minute increments, going for $150 per dose? I don't begrudge the therapist his livelihood, but "unconditional" his regard is not.

We, on the other hand, had vowed to love each other "for richer or for poorer, in sickness and in health." And as eternal soulmates, we now sweetened the package with a lifetime emotional benefit: By communicating ever more cleanly, ever less defensively, we would love our way to the bottom of every conflict. Unraveling and dissipating, in the process, wounds and grievances from our distant, individual pasts.

The Eternal Soulmate's Stick

But we also saw the marriage contract as a license to call (confront) the energy, whenever we sensed something, behavioral or *pre*-behavioral, disturbing our own equilibrium. As the one who bore the brunt of our partner's neurotic habit, we considered it both our right and our duty to initiate process. In sharp contrast to the therapist's more passive objectivity, our job was precisely to personalize every marital interaction—to insist our spouse take notice of her energy's impact *on us.* To thereby make our presence—and through it, every latent (individual) conflict—truly felt.

That meant never hesitating to probe our partner's defenses in order to give our love the chance to do its healing work. As suggested above, we saw this as the growth-demanding ingredient that was missing from the professional therapeutic relationship.

Of course, doing this cleanly, i.e., knowing *whose* defenses were actually asserting themselves on any given occasion, was much easier said than done. For in establishing the relational homeostasis, we'd learned precisely how to push each other's neurotic hot-buttons. Our mission—to express more love and less pathology—thus became, by definition, an ongoing exercise in self-examination. It was in this way that the individual and relational processes truly catalyzed one another.

For we were determined to do more than just identify our neuroses. We were going to *grow* ourselves *and* the relationship. Or move on to find the one with whom we might realize such individual and relational synergy.

10

Sexual Awareness

A passage in the Talmud reads, *"Da lifney mi ata omeyd"*— "Know (be aware) before Whom you are standing." This text often appears on or near the Ark, in the synagogue. The concept is, we should live our lives as though always standing before the Holy Ark—knowing that our every act and thought are fully open to God's view.

It was on our initial visit to the community, before we'd decided to move to Normal, that I was confronted with the practical implications of standing, not before God, but before someone with a paranormally intimate view of me. "Take your filthy hands off my daughter and *keep* them off!" Tanya upbraided me.

Now I hadn't physically touched Tanya's attractive teenage daughter but was as guilty as Jimmy Carter of the lustful thought. This rebuke was my notice Tanya ran a tight ship when it came to sexual energy in particular. Since most of us were used to giving our fantasies free rein, her psychic sensitivity on this score made us nervous and kept us vigilant.

The realization that our sexuality could be observed, even in the absence of the slightest verbal or behavioral "come on," cast a whole new light on our social mores. We began to notice how much sexual communication takes place long before rising to the level of suggestive speech or body language. Our liberated culture has gone almost completely unconscious in this regard. As Dillon used to put it, the same man who might shoot you for touching his car thinks nothing of it when you dance cheek to cheek with his wife!

But Tanya's zero tolerance for energetic smut was practical, not prudish. Considering the level to which we were holding each other accountable, we could hardly have overlooked foreign sexual incursions into the eternal soulmate relationship. It would have been the height of duplicity to ask another member of the group to process with me—to lower his emotional guard—while I was entertaining sexual fantasies about his wife!

Or to be having sex with my own wife while thinking about someone else's. Indeed, we considered it the spouse's job to ferret out any such energetic philandering. If my partner didn't care where my consciousness was (so long as my sex organ was present and accounted for), *both* of us were being energetically unfaithful.

For our goal was to stop using anyone—from the total stranger to our own spouse—as a sex object. In the case of the spouse, that might mean initiating process even at the cost of *coitus interruptus*. In the case of an attractive young stranger, it meant envisioning her mother and father, standing beside her . . . loving her in a more personal way than I might, in their absence, have been inclined to.

"Da," they'd be saying if I would only hear them. "Know before Whom you are standing."

11

Group Psychoanalysis

Diane's experience in psychoanalysis made the consolidation of individual, conjoint and group modalities all the more attractive to us. I'll digress here to describe the psychoanalytic model of emotional healing, as I've come to understand it.

The analyst (usually an M.D. psychiatrist) "treats" the patient in an interpersonally sanitized, clinical environment. Lying on a couch, the patient free-associates (says whatever comes to mind), with a minimum of direction from the analyst. The idea is for the patient, over time, to get in touch with his innermost fantasies and preoccupations.

The analyst, by contrast, remains scrupulously *im*personal in these sessions. Seated behind the patient, like an invisible alter ego, he offers sporadic interpretive comments, the substance and timing of which are what make the process a therapeutic one. But like any good clinician, the analyst monitors the patient's process from a personal/relational remove.

There's good reason for this professional detachment. The symptomatology of the patient's "illness" is his history of unsatisfactory interactions with family, friends, employers, etc. However well handled the analyst's own issues and relationships might be, were he to allow his emotional field to intersect the patient's, he'd become part of the very subject matter he was trying to help sort out.

To prevent this, the analyst takes pains to avoid contact with the patient outside their formal sessions. He likewise cordons himself off from the patient's family and friends, in order to maintain complete confidentiality (and undivided loyalty).

The analytic hour thus amounts to an interactive time out for the patient—a freeze-framing of emotionally charged events for review and interpretation, before pushing the relational resume-play button. To that end, *both* participants are sequestered from their respective personal contexts, for a most private but relationally sterile *tete à tete*.

Now I didn't know any of the above in the days of Diane's first psychoanalytic attempt. However, all the signals my wife was sending suggested her treatment wasn't going well. Over a period of months, she'd become increasingly depressed, to the point she was talking, albeit abstractly, of *suicide*. When this got me concerned enough to begin hiding away my razor blades, I took it upon myself to phone her analyst.

Dr. Heinrich spoke to me in terms even a psychologically illiterate young lawyer would comprehend: "Sir, you and I do not have a contract. My contract is with your wife. I cannot discuss this matter with you. So please don't interfere any further in my work with Diane."

Even with my current understanding of the importance of confidentiality in the psychotherapeutic relationship, this response to my legitimate if unsolicited concern strikes me as doctrinaire and overzealous. My reaction at the time was to give Diane an ultimatum: "You can have your 'work' with that man or your marriage with me. In present circumstances, if the good doctor interprets my call as an interference with *his* contractual expectations, one of us has got to go."

Thus forced to choose one authority figure over the other, Diane chose me. The implications of this will be addressed in a later chapter, but the above may shed further light on the appeal Tanya and Sherman's approach had for both of us.

For in their community, there was no turf war between the individual and relational processes. The relationship was seen as the very portal to the psychodynamics of the individual. Whatever issues needed to be addressed, it was within the relationship that they'd inevitably present. We could then work backwards, from the patent marital conflicts to the more latent individual ones.

Tanya and Sherman were thus taking a systems approach, examining the individual issues in their larger, relational context. But unlike a systems-oriented therapist or marriage counselor, they had on-the-spot access to the relationship and its constituents. If a conflict erupted at midnight, we'd all roll out of bed and lend our collective insight to its resolution. And we'd stay with the process until the energy at play was identified and had shifted.

Needless to say, this created quite a different culture than the one we'd all grown up with. In normal married life, husbands and wives attempt to address their conflicts, if at all, in private. So long as the marital *behavior* remains within bounds, the relationship muddles through its ups and downs, maintaining discretion when on public display. An unfinished argument on Saturday afternoon will give way to convivial chitchat as the dinner guests arrive. Unless and until the pair can no longer keep the lid on, they'll endure this marital schizophrenia, relating to each other one way when they're alone and quite another (like a set of dress clothes) for public consumption.

In the community, we came to disparage the latter as "performance behavior." Our goal was to walk our domestic talk—to live up to the authenticity we espoused, not just at home, but in our social and even economic contexts.

But we didn't do much socializing outside our circle. And economically, we were resting on our collective if fast dwindling laurels. In short, we'd retreated from the very settings that tend to call for performance behavior in the first place.

In the vernacular of personal boundaries, we had all but erased them among ourselves but erected a firm, parochial one between us and the world at large. Like provoked bees, we'd swarm in at the first sign of non-communicative backsliding within our ranks. (We considered this a form of communal "tough love.") But in the larger scheme of things, we'd severed the umbilical cord of socioeconomic accountability that makes life on earth what it is.

I recall one time we did venture out into the real world. Through an acquaintance on the faculty at Purdue, Diane and I were invited to lead a ten-week pilot program of group therapy for couples. This was under the auspices of the University's Center for Family Studies. The project went so well, several of the couples wanted to keep working with us after the formal program had ended. So we started seeing them at our home, on a weekly basis.

Unfortunately, one of the true zealots of the community took a reading of our energy and concluded we were becoming uppity in our new roles. Our home office was a room that served, when we weren't meeting with the outsiders, as passageway to the laundry room. Unwilling to be inconvenienced by the airs she perceived us to be putting on, this woman came barging through one of our sessions with her basket of dirty underwear (giving a whole new meaning to "airing our dirty linens").

We should have realized then that the gap between the community's uncompromising agenda and the demands of life in the real world was too great to bridge. That authenticity and discretion aren't mutually exclusive—personal boundaries not an all-or-nothing proposition. And that communication can be both honest and sincere without being unrelentingly self-revealing or conflictual.

12

Ego

At one introductory trance circle, a young woman asked Dillon if he could help her become a famous photographer. "You're already famous with me," Dillon quipped; "I don't know what more I could possibly do for you in the 'fame' department."

Dillon never encouraged our thrust for personal status, much less fame. He posited "ego"* as our spiritual nemesis and exhorted us to "overcome" it.

I was thinking about this one day as I waited at the Department of Motor Vehicles to renew my license. After twenty minutes in line, I got close enough to the counter to read that the renewal fee had gone up, from $4 to $7. I had $6 in my pocket, and my checkbook. But the sign also announced that they'd stopped taking checks.

It was a hot summer day, and I was tired and fed up. The last thing I wanted to do was drive all the way home and back, just to wait another twenty minutes in line. In my prior, more dignified life, there would have been no alternative.

---

*I use the term (as did Dillon) in the colloquial, not the Freudian sense.

But my ruminations about ego now ripened into a bold if unconventional action plan: Why not ask one of the fifty other patrons in line if they'd save me an hour's time by lending me the dollar I was short. (I would mail it back to them or, if they preferred, write them a personal check.)

The thought of doing this threw me into immediate agitation and embarrassment. Was my resistance to so practical a solution something I should endeavor to "overcome"? I turned to the person behind me and simply described my predicament.

A woman standing distinctly off to the side quickly pulled a dollar from her purse, rushed over and handed it to me. When I began to write her a check, she emphatically put up her hand, stating: *"I have been told* that I should give you this money—that it's important. Under the circumstances, it wouldn't be right for me to accept your check."

Now, it could just be that a disproportionate percentage of Normal's population *isn't.* But I preferred to take meaning from what had just transpired: that Dillon (or some other privy to my internal process) had gotten the attention of my flesh and blood benefactor. Who, in turn, was willing to underwrite a buck's worth of my spiritual education.

More was accomplished here, in my estimation, than the avoidance of a drive home to get the extra dollar.

13

"The Universe Will Provide" (and Other Euphemisms of Denial)

Experiences such as the above convinced me that virtually any interaction could serve either to dilute or to reinforce my identification with ego. When I hid my distress from those who hurt me, I chose defensiveness over honest communication. When I allowed the fear of rejection to deter me from asking for help, I fostered ego at the expense of relationship and faith in God.

But this seemed a slippery slope. Was there not a line to be drawn between faith and humility, on one hand, and slothful dependency, on the other? Otherwise, what kept us all (in the name of "trusting the process") from just plunking ourselves down in some comfortable spot—with a sign reading, "Vulnerable. Need Cash. God Bless"?

We did that for a while, in a manner of speaking. It wasn't as if we hadn't put our own, hard-earned money where our spiritual mouths were. But somewhere along the way, we lost sight of the fact that neither our marriages nor our spirituality existed in a physical (or fiscal) vacuum. Compounding the error, as our cash and credit resources dwindled over months of non-remunerative interpersonal process, we became self-righteous about our very willingness to turn to others for help.

I remember, for instance, a conversation with a fellow who'd attended a number of the early Chicago trance circles. Brian had stopped short of moving with us to Normal but lent $5,000 to Ed and Jessica, to help them make the move. Now, reasonably enough, he wanted to be paid back. And since the debtors were living in my house, it fell to me, as head of household, to monitor the financial and interpersonal heat we were starting to get.

So on Brian's next visit to Normal, I arranged a sit-down for the four of us. He opened the discussion with a rendition of his new mantra, "a contract is a contract." We, of course, weren't interested in the law of contracts but in the deeper energies at play.

I told Brian there were two ways we could approach this conversation. "Contractually speaking," the debtors had a duty to repay the money, and he had every right to collect it (rights and duties being the correlatives of such obligation-driven, i.e., legal relations). But Ed, Jessica, Diane and I had moved beyond such bourgeois concerns to a more personal (if all but unenforceable) "commitment"-driven relationship. This meant we'd stopped focusing on the petty details of who owed what to whom in favor of a richer interactive process. Into which I was now inviting Brian, also, to step.

The closing pitch went something like this:

We can sign a formal agreement, by which we'll undertake to pay you so much per month, for so many months. If we don't live up to the terms, you can get in line with our other creditors—or file your lawsuit.

Or we can give you the kind of commitment we've made to each other. The essence of which is, we're accountable [another spiritual term of art] for what we do each day and how we disburse the financial fruits thereof. Were you to become part of that ongoing discussion, we'd owe you a real voice in our deliberations, financial and otherwise.

I'd be willing to speak to you not just on the monthly basis we deal with our creditors, but daily. I'd welcome you into our soul searching as to which financial need is most compelling at any given moment. By engaging with us in that process, you might get paid back sooner or you might get paid back later than if we go the route of contractual obligation.

The difference is that accountability addresses *all* our needs and resources (yours included). But under the obligation scenario, the $5,000 Ed and Jessica owe you will delimit your relationship with them . . . and with the rest of us.

The upshot was, Brian decided to be our brother instead of our creditor.

Yet I was also willing to play the patsy of my own spiritual fast-talk. There was the time Tony and Lisa were living in our house, with their three-year-old daughter and another child on the way. Tony had just gotten a job at the post office, sorting mail on the graveyard shift. I'd encouraged him to apply for that job; in fact, I'd put up the money for the course that got him through the qualifying exam. (And for the new tricycle his little girl had her heart set on for Christmas.)

But at dinner one cold January evening, Tony shared with us how much he hated the new job. He threw in that his coworkers were plying him with amphetamines, just to get him through the nightly shift.

Now I'd known this young man since moving to the community and did feel a sense of commitment to him and his family. But it was our mortgage, not theirs, inching closer to foreclosure. So what I felt like saying was:

YOUR JOB SATISFACTION'S NOT MY PROB-LEM. *LIFE'S A BITCH!* NOW **STRAIGHTEN UP AND FLY RIGHT**. And I'd better see your family's share of our expenses without fail on the 15th!

But before I could get that out, I happened to glance at his little girl, playing serenely on the floor with our own toddler-son. Those two were inseparable. I couldn't help but imagine the turn her life might take were her daddy to get hooked on speed.

"To hell with that job," I heard myself saying. "We'll figure out another way for you to bring in some money."

During this confusing time, I learned what it was like to walk into a supermarket and see items I wanted to buy but couldn't afford. One day, I was in Chicago, filing a brief, when I realized I might not have enough *gasoline* money to make it back to Normal. "I can't live this way," I whined that evening. "I'm a *lawyer*, for Christ's sake. I shouldn't have to hassle over whether it takes $2 or $3 worth of gas to get me home from court!"

Tanya glared at me. *"All my life,"* she seethed, "I've been 'hassling' over things like that. What's it *like,* Mr. Lawyer, to just say, *'fill 'er up'?"*

Driving to Chicago a week later, I was pleased to find I had money for gas and for lunch in the bargain. "Where shall I eat?" I asked myself. "Chinese sounds good," came the answer. "If you pass a Chinese restaurant, PULL IN."

Seconds later, I spotted a place I'd never tried, the New Hong Kong Buffet. As I entered, there seated at the table just in front of me was my erstwhile boss and current part-time employer, Jack Murphy.

Now I'd known and worked for Jack for several years but never shared a meal alone with him. He seemed preoccupied and rather somber. Taking some liberty, I asked him what was up. "It's a money thing," he replied.

Flashing back to my recent experiences with creditors and at the Department of Motor Vehicles, I matter-of-factly suggested Jack just come right out with his predicament to whatever employees or business associates stood to be affected. Making a great leap which, in my spiritual oblivion, seemed like no leap at all, I told him, "If the firm was a *family,* you'd just round us all up and say, 'Uncle Jack's got a problem.'"

Jack seemed to shrug off the suggestion. But I left that restaurant no less puffed up—convinced that God had sent me there to deliver a spiritual message! That I'd just done, for Jack Murphy, what the woman at the DMV had done for me.

14

Whom Do You Love?

At one trance circle, I told Mr. Dillon I was feeling confused about life's purpose . . . more particularly, my own. I wondered what I was missing—if I was even asking the right questions.

"Do you love your wife?" Dillon responded, seeming to change the subject.

"Yes," I answered, after a brief pause.

"Then what else is there to ask . . . or to know?"

The ultimate purpose of life, Dillon seemed to be saying, was to love—not in some abstract, agape sense, but in relation to another specific human being. His spiritual teaching thus differed from the Eastern philosophies I'd encountered. The latter discouraged relational entanglements, viewing them as distractions from what should be the aspirant's single-minded yearning for God.

But Dillon posited relationship as an ideal venue within which to develop our spirituality. He saw the householder's worldly responsibilities as a natural hedge against selfishness. Our very entanglements should help inoculate us against hedonism—preventing sensation from drowning out all receptivity to the needs of our significant others.

My own father sired four children and was married to the same woman for 51 years. But he never repented of his hedonism. When the issue of his drinking occasionally came up, his defense was that he didn't "have" to drink but rather *chose* to.

Now did the fact he could say such a thing mean he didn't love us? Or was he "doing the best he could?" And did our willingness to continue interacting with him, long after we'd reached ages at which we had a choice in the matter, mean we loved him more than he loved us? Or were we co-dependent gluttons for punishment, no less choosing relation with him than he was choosing his alcohol over us?

We'll all put up with more mistreatment from family members than from a stranger on the bus. More from our boss than our neighbor. The question always reduces to, "What have we to gain and what to lose by the continuation or termination of this relationship?"

Most of the time, these deliberations are subconscious. But one interaction with my father, shortly before we left the community, taught me to deal more forthrightly with the perennial question, "Is this relationship redeemable? Should I risk further pain for the possibility of experiencing love with this person?"

My 1983 taxes were in arrears, and the IRS had now placed a lien on our house. I knew my dad had some money saved up. What about asking him for some help?

The likelihood of a positive response seemed remote— that of a contemptuous rebuke, all but certain. But it had been a long time since I'd asked Dad for anything (other than to sober up). Suppose I were to approach him, this time, about my predicament instead of his own. With the kind of straightforwardness I'd summoned for the patrons at the Department of Motor Vehicles.

There was a big difference, of course, between that interaction and the one now under consideration. My father and I had a history. It's probably easier to stand on the corner and beg from strangers than to confront our more personal demons by approaching "our own" for help.

But the good fairy was nudging me to take this risk—to give my dad and myself one more opportunity to grow, both individually and relationally. Her challenge went something like this:

What if God is standing by, ready to support (but not initiate) a miracle. Waiting to give your father the gentle boost he needs if you can just approach him nonjudgmentally. With the common respect he's not been shown in years, especially by a member of his own family.

Imagine the potential healing if he could then find the wherewithal to part with some of his false security. Not because he "had" to—not because you demanded it. Because he *chose* to. Because, in the light of your vulnerability, his love unexpectedly surged ahead of his fear.

And think what such an outcome would mean to you. Getting the IRS off your back would be the least of it. This isn't some stranger at the DMV—this one's *your* daddy (who already *is* addicted). But that sober reality needn't deny him (or you) the opportunity to rise to the occasion.

"Don't be a shmuck," the bad fairy cut in. "The reason beggars stand on street corners is, they know better than to beat their heads against a stone wall. You'd be smarter to join them than to call your father—you might actually raise some cash! In all events, the rejection of a passing stranger would be a lot less painful than one more kick in the teeth from *that* asshole."

The good fairy won. I made the call. My dad was sober. So far so good. I spoke to him with more emotional reality than I had since early childhood. And he listened, with uncharacteristic patience.

After a few moments' discussion, Dad said: "Here's what I want you to do. You call the IRS and arrange to pay them $300 a month for the next two years. I can't give you any of my saved-up money. But I'll send half my Social Security check, and you can use that to pay off the IRS."

That conversation was a miracle I cherish to this day. But in the mail, a few days later, came the following note: "I can't do it. It's *not* that I don't love you. Please understand."

I burst into tears when I read the above. But I also knew this communication was a second miracle, equal to the first. It had been a long time since my dad and I had offered our best to each other. Since we'd both found the wherewithal to acknowledge our love . . . in the very *face* of our limitations.

15

The End of the Beginning

The rabbis of the Talmud used to say, *"Im eyn kemach, eyn Torah"*– "Without bread, there can *be* no spirituality." This is a lesson our community never grasped. Instead of all going out and getting full-time jobs, we lurched from one financial crisis to another. Our still intense, still important communal processes felt increasingly like they were taking place on the deck of the Titanic.

But this was the roaring '80s, when the banks were falling all over themselves to lend money. Each time I became convinced the ship really was going down, a letter would arrive, informing me that in light of my "excellent payment history," my credit line was being increased. (And on each such occasion, I'd ask myself whether this was God, throwing me another lifeline, or Satan, luring me farther out to sea.)

Having come this far, I don't believe I'd have given up on the community based on our financial distress, standing alone. But two other issues arose, in the face of which it became impossible for me to remain part of Tanya and Sherman's camp.

The first was ideological. A senior member of the group announced, with their apparent blessing, that he was leaving his wife. Her lagging spiritual progress was preventing him from realizing his own fullest potential. So he'd decided "to put God and spiritual purpose first"—even though Dillon himself had pronounced this couple "eternal soulmates."

When presented with this development, Dillon rewrote, on the spot, our most fundamental tenet. Such inability of soulmates to progress together was exceedingly rare, he declared gravely. But under the circumstances, he could arrange to have the eternal relationship effectively annulled.

This facile revision of our whole psychospiritual philosophy cast every other assumption about what we were doing together into significant doubt. If a spiritually ordained, eternal soulmate relationship could fail, even after the enlightened and intensive care we'd all given it, something was seriously amiss.

How could such a contradiction be so blithely rationalized by Dillon (and accepted by Tanya and Sherman)? And if a senior member of the group could so summarily dump his own eternal soulmate, what must that say about the commitment he'd only derivatively made to me and mine?

The final straw was a confrontation between Sherman and me. As a follow-up to the couples counseling Diane and I had done at Purdue, she was asked to teach a formal course in family dynamics. This time, she invited not just me but Tanya and Sherman to team-teach the course with her.

True to our convictions, we structured the course around the theme of honest communication within the family. So I shouldn't have been surprised when, a month or two into the semester, one of the students took me aside and invited me to walk my talk. He asked me why Diane and I seemed to defer, at every turn, to Tanya and Sherman. "They appear to be *controlling* you," the student boldly asserted.

This young man was obviously going way out on a limb to make such a statement. He knew nothing of our history with Tanya and Sherman and had no apparent axe to grind. "We defer out of respect for their insight and experience," I tentatively responded.

But when I recounted the above on the way home from class, Sherman's reaction all but made the student's case. "You betrayed me," he declared, with little affect and less circumspection. "You should have acknowledged me forthrightly as your spiritual teacher. And told the student that as such, it was fine with you to be controlled by me."

We rode the rest of the way home in stunned silence. I waited a few days for the dust to settle, hoping Sherman would get in touch with just how out of control his ego had become. Instead, the standoff escalated.

The family that had been sharing our home abruptly gathered up its belongings and moved out. This without benefit of five minutes' process, though we'd endured countless hours of tortured soul-searching with them over the most trifling issues of daily life.

The man who'd quit his night job at the post office with my blessing now refused to let his little daughter *play* with our toddler son. A woman who'd been nursemaid and aunt to our infant removed her coffee maker and dishtowels from our house. And never held our baby again.

The weeks and months that followed were the bitterest of our lives. I've weighed, long and hard, my gains, losses, choices and responsibility for all I experienced in the community. Whether I could have learned what I learned there at less personal cost, I cannot say.

I know only that the above incident shattered my illusion of accountability with this group of people. And that any further growth there would not have been worth the price.

PART THREE

WORKING
WITHOUT A NET

16

Two Little Pigs

Looking back on this difficult time, I believe my greatest challenge was to separate the wheat from the chaff of the preceding three years. But our first priority was to re-establish diplomatic relations with our "blood" families—if they'd have us back. And I'd have to explain myself to Jack Murphy, in the hope I still had a full-time job to return to.

While packing up for our move back to the city, I came across some correspondence to my older brother, in which I'd attempted to summarize just what we thought we were doing in Normal:

Dear Frank,

One of the things I so admire about Murphy and Green is their open-mindedness about the lifestyle we've opted for. The day I told Murphy I wanted to go part-time, he held his calls for twenty minutes to hear my saga of moving to Normal, our relationship to the community gathered here and the circumstances that had brought me to this decision. I told him about Mr. Dillon and the influence he's had on our marriage and values. Then I steeled myself for the expected skeptical, if not outright disparaging response.

After hearing me out, Murphy squared himself in his seat, locking me eyeball to eyeball. "You know, Adam, if you'd told me all this shit the first day you walked into this office . . . " Jack paused to spit a mouthful of tobacco into his cup, and I clutched the sides of my chair, waiting for the other shoe to drop . . . "we'd still be sitting here having this conversation."

I appreciated Murphy's gesture and regretted not having been more candid with him at our initial meeting. Of course, I'd never lied to him about anything; I'd just talked about wanting to live in a smaller town, etc.—the same rationales we gave you for the move to Normal. It seems time, now, to let you in on the rest of the story:

*Diane and I came here (1) to work on our relationship, which, after twelve years, was hanging by a thread. We hoped to make a fresh start, this time putting the marriage ahead of everything else; (2) to learn to **be** more authentic, first and foremost, with each other. That meant getting a handle on neurotic behaviors, the unconscious as well as the conscious, that have dominated our communication for most of our married life; (3) to enhance our self-awareness (bringing the unconscious **into** consciousness), by trusting our feelings the way we've previously trusted only thoughts and opinions. (From this perspective, the heart has more to offer than the mind, and loving trumps "telling it like it is."); (4) to share our personal and relational process with others, similarly com-*

mitted, thereby creating an extended family environment for ourselves and our son;* (5) to share, also, our material things, in the hope of outgrowing our selfishness; (6) to overcome petty ego, trading the illusion of gross control for a subtler, less provincial sense of purpose. In short: (7) to put more faith in God, realizing that our success only seems to spring from credentials, worry, manipulation and being in the right place at the right time.

I could hear the wheels of your mind squeaking, louder as you moved from number one to number seven—perhaps by that one lumping us with the Moonies, or whomever. The truth, in all events, is that we believe in God. And while that, in itself, isn't news, we now try to glean spiritual content from the most prosaic of our experience. That is how we express and nourish our nascent faith.

Frank, I've been afraid to share such aspirations with you in the past. Part of my process here seems a weaning from whatever has so deterred me. I guess I haven't wanted to hear you accuse me of being "in need of professional help."

Which of these tenets would I still claim were I writing Frank today, from the carnage of our failed utopian experiment? And in approaching him now, would I concede that he'd been right to condemn it?

I found and re-read his letter answering the above:

* We came to Normal with one son but left with three.

Adam,

There's a difference between being open-minded and empty-headed. I think your current lifestyle follows the pattern you established earlier of chasing after false gods and relying on phony "support" groups for "love and guidance." Sorry, but I believe problems related to self-image/self-respect are best dealt with in a one-to-one relationship with a competent psychiatrist.

This is not an "accusation"; it's loving, caring, sound counsel. Healthy individuals don't need nor desire to "share" such intimacies as you describe with groups. People—healthy, emotionally mature people —establish appropriate boundaries.

I'm struck by the vague psychobabble that threads its way through your letter, e.g., the "illusion of control" and "the heart has more to offer than the mind." Your dogma is, of course, anti-reason precisely because it is unreasonable!

*But of your seven tenets, the last two concern me the most—because you, my brother, aren't "overcoming" ego, you're **wallowing** in it; and because healthy people don't give over their control—not to gurus, ghosts, groups or gods—not to **anyone**—not **ever!** It's when we abandon our own reason and are content to rely on external authority that trouble begins.*

I share these feelings with you because I care about you and want to see you grow up already and take charge of your own life. Bertrand Russell wrote:

"There is something feeble and a little contemptible about a man who cannot face the perils of life without the help of comfortable myths. Almost inevitably, some part of him is aware that they are myths and that he believes them only because they are comforting. But he dare not face this thought! Moreover, since he is aware, however dimly, that his opinions are not rational, he becomes furious when they are disputed."

*Adam, you are so intelligent, articulate and gifted. Get some **real** help for the emotional needs. As they say around here, "Wake up and smell the coffee!" And spare me the spiritual sloganeering—don't engage me in polemics. I can't validate your mishoogas!**

> *Love,*
> *Your brother, Frank*

As I read the above today, I see both the love and the wisdom in my brother's message (though I still chafe at his rigidity in the face of my *mishoogas*). But my response at the time was just as Bertrand Russell had predicted:

Dear Frank,

I'll try to keep my polemics to a minimum. The difference between us is that you view belief in God as unreasonable, immature and a symptom of mental illness. If there is a God, what could possibly be unhealthy about wanting to subordinate one's personal will to His? On the other hand, what's so admirable,

---

* Yiddish for nonsense (craziness).

responsible and healthy about "establishing appropriate boundaries" (with everyone but the recommended psychiatrist), while remaining spiritually illiterate?

You sing the praises of psychiatry, which you've not experienced, while condemning the spirit, which you've also not experienced. If that's not the height of presumptuousness, I'm definitely wallowing in something.

Your brother, Adam

P. S. **Fuck** *Bertrand Russell.*

As I'll relate in a later chapter, I've long since obtained the recommended one-on-one with the competent psychiatrist. I'm fairly confident the good doctor would today give me a decent bill of mental health. But will my brother nevertheless conclude, from all I've written here, that I'm still to be counted among the purveyors of psychobabble? (And what would Bertrand Russell say?)

However our relationship may continue to unfold, in 1986, I had to call on Frank for financial help to get me back on my feet. I felt like the little pig who had built with sticks, importuning the one who'd built with bricks. Some part of me dimly sensed that I'd laid some solid, if half-baked bricks of my own. But for the present, they were affording my family and me no shelter and little comfort.

17

Practice Makes Perfect

We thus swallowed more pride and gratefully accepted help from both my brothers, my sister, my mother and Diane's parents. I went back to Murphy & Green and was relieved to find their door still open to me.

At the firm over the next few years, I kept my nose to the grindstone, reassuring my employers I still had what it took professionally. I outlasted the jibes about searching for "higher authorities" and resumed the persona of the scholarly if eccentric legal analyst and writer. I got good results on some complex cases, published an article in the Loyola Law Journal and stood poised to reclaim my professional *bona fides*.

But some part of me, unrepentant of my past and uncertain of my worldly direction, found it difficult to confine myself to the straight and narrow of professional life. I was frustrated by the limited occasion it was affording me for interaction with other human beings.

This may come as a surprise to those whose image of lawyers derives from the O.J. Simpson trial. The fact is, even "litigators" spend most of their time sequestered at their desks, poring over documents of one sort or another.

There are scores of these hours for every one spent in lively, argumentative banter.

In addition, most lawyers tend toward emotional reticence. This is partly a function of the law's emphasis on analytical skills. It is, after all, our ability as thinkers, not as feelers, for which we're remunerated. Nevertheless, while I hardly expected the kind of self-revealing processes that had been the staple of my interactive diet in the community, I found the paucity of non-legal communication among lawyers to be the other end of the interpersonal spectrum.

The time came for me to be considered for partnership. This is, in law firm culture, what tenure is in academia. Partnership would thus place the firm's (and, by extension, the legal community's) imprimatur on my professional achievements. Given the slow if scenic career path I'd taken, I craved the recognition and sense of identity that "making partner" would finally afford me.

But my dissatisfaction with the interpersonal pedestrianism of law practice (and, perhaps, my inability to let things go too smoothly for too long) got the better of me. It thus occurred to me I might be happier as a judge than I'd been as an attorney.

It also happened, just at that time, that there were an unusual number of openings on the Cook County Circuit Court. I had some political contacts in the Governor's office (where those appointments would be made). But the current administration was also nearing the end of its term.

This put me in a kind of "catch 22." To be a viable candidate, I'd need strong support from my current employers, Jack Murphy and Jack Green. But this was hardly the time to be discussing with them my desire to be working somewhere else! If such candor were to cost me my partnership, it might dash, at the same stroke, any prospect I had for appointment to the bench.

As I ruminated on this dilemma, it struck me that this was the same moment (another layer of the onion) I'd faced when applying for the job at Murphy & Green in the first place. Would I share any more of myself now than I had then? Or would I be hearing Jack Murphy say, down the road, "Of course we'll support you for judge; but if you'd told us two years ago that you aspired to the bench, we'd still have voted you in"?

Thus determined to practice what I'd preached in the letter to my brother Frank, I concluded that making partner was of little value if it required me to stifle my legitimate conflicts and ambitions. So I requested a meeting with Jack Murphy, Jack Green and the head of the firm's litigation section, Kevin O'Reilly.

They did question my commitment to the firm in the light of my interest in the bench. But the discussion was fair, frank and healthy. Afterwards, I tried to capture the essence of our conversation in the following:

MEMORANDUM

TO: *JLM, JJG and KMO*

FROM: *AE*

DATE: *June 16, 1989*

Re: *Partnership and Commitment*

Just a few more thoughts about the "commitment" my pending partnership has brought to issue. For me, this isn't just about the financial responsibility/opportunity a partnership implies. Titles notwithstanding, we've done a decent job, these last few years, keeping food on our respective tables. Having tested and gotten to know one another to that extent, I'd like, now, to up the ante–to move the discussion beyond the breadwinning per se.

So when Jack M. says he needs partners "who will be there to share the load with him," I frankly think there's a deeper statement he's trying to make. Isn't partnership about committing to one another personally—i.e., to be working for each other's success as an end in itself (obviously while pursuing our own success)?

What I'm saying is that "financial commitment" is an oxymoron. We've all got financial obligations; but "commitment" is something personal. People who are with you for economic advantage, however mutual, will be gone the moment their self-interest so dictates. So if you ever are left holding the bag, it will be because you had "partners" who were obligated to you but not personally committed.

This isn't just semantics. Loyalty is a function of relationship in a way that promises, agreements, even performance are not. The most unpleasant part of becoming your partner has been the task of convincing you I'm the productive equal of this or that person. Such internal competitiveness may get you a

*collection of brilliant lawyers, trial lawyers, rain-
makers and worker bees, but it doesn't engender loyalty. For once the rainmaker convinces you (and himself) that he **is** a rainmaker, why should he stay and
make rain **with you**?*

*Jack G. was right: Our discussion was less about
my desire to be a judge than my need to say these
things to you three. Relationship and prosperity
aren't mutually exclusive, and I've got no bone to
pick with financial security as a goal. (As Jack M.
aptly put it, we wouldn't be beating our brains out
together if we were all rich instead of argumentative.)*

*But if you decide you want me around for the long
term, be prepared for me to affect more than just your
economic bottom line. And if you're telling me "not
to go there" with your 19 existing partners, I've got
to know I can, at the very least, with you three guys.*

I probably expended thirty non-billable hours on this effort to articulate, in the seemingly unreceptive environment
of a busy law practice, ideals that had become part of me in
the community. Kevin O'Reilley, who was valedictorian of
his law school class, claimed not to understand a word of
the above. Nevertheless, he canceled a trip out of town to
be there for the partners' meeting at which I'd be voted in
or out . . . and spearheaded the effort in my behalf.

I did also apply for the bench. But the commission that
vets judicial candidates for the Governor couldn't get past
my recent stint as a spiritual communist. My interview
seemed to go much more smoothly the second time I ap-
plied (the community never even came up).

"Yeah," Jack Murphy quipped when I still didn't make the cut. "They must have powwowed before you got there: 'Here comes the nut case . . . let's not rile him!'"

18

Process and Prosperity

My pre-partnership memo and related conversations weren't the first time I'd presumed to smuggle interpersonal process into the professional workings of Murphy & Green. When I first joined the firm, in 1983, three other recruits had come aboard at the same time. That being the case, Jack and Jack had left it to us to determine the order in which our names would appear on the letterhead.

Our foursome consisted of two recent graduates (one of whom had just finished clerking for the firm), a lawyer who'd practiced for several years in another state, and me, with more gray hair than all the others combined. Someone suggested we draw straws and be done with this uncomfortable business. I said I was fine with that but suggested we first take a few minutes, over lunch, to find out whether any of our names *should* come ahead of the others on the letterhead.

The woman who had clerked for the firm suggested such tenure might entitle her to seniority for letterhead purposes. The other recent grad countered that having himself clerked at one of Chicago's larger, more established firms, his decision to join the young upstarts, Murphy & Green, had astounded his peers. So he'd assured them that within a few years, they'd see his name right up near the *top* of the much shorter, M & G letterhead.

"Leapfrogging the three of you would get me off to a terrific start!" he enthused. Then, in a more pensive tone, he added, "and it would impress the *hell* out of my father."

The lawyer who'd practiced in another state was also quite candid. As it turned out, he didn't much care where his name turned up on the letterhead. But he fretted so passive a stance, were it to leave the room, might cause Murphy to question his adversarial zeal!

I had no quarrel with the points my colleagues had raised. So I suggested my name come last. And that they carry on without me to arrive at the proper order for theirs.

Pandemonium ensued. You'd have thought I'd pulled out a revolver and pointed it at my temple! It became a matter of utmost urgency to talk me out of my position, lest the others be perceived as having taken unfair *advantage* of me.

In the face of this uproar, and realizing the lunch hour was almost over, I volunteered to break the logjam by going *first* on the letterhead. We all had a good laugh, then proceeded to draw straws.

The meeting thus concluded with the same result (and yet a totally different feeling) than if we'd just drawn straws in the first place. I don't remember the order in which our names ended up. Fifteen years later, I'm the only one of the four still on the letterhead (which today, in all events, is alphabetical). But I do know no one left that meeting feeling short-changed by the outcome.

Looking back on these, my prime breadwinning years, it occurs to me that "climbing the letterhead" meant no more (and no less) than squaring my lofty pronouncements with my own productivity, on a sustainable basis. When all is said and done, that's what walking one's talk means in the business and professional world.

And what of those whose economic fate was also riding on my effort to integrate what I'd learned in the community with my real-world obligations? In those years, I made them my safety net. Before embarking on any interactive course that threatened to impact us financially, I'd convene a family meeting to ascertain whether my wife and children were *with* me in the proposed course of action.

I'd lay out all the risks, like the hospital does when you go in for surgery. I'd ask each son what he thought I should do—and whether he was willing to absorb his share of the economic blow if things went badly. In that way, the memo to Jack, Jack and Kevin was not from me alone, but from me, Diane and my boys.

19

Worrying Wisely

"Worry is the worst murderer of mankind," Mr. Dillon used to declare. Pop-psychology and New-Age culture likewise tend to demonize stress, implying that the more we worry, the sicker we become (until, eventually, we *die* of something). But Dillon was also fond of reminding us that "there *is* no death and there are no dead." In that case, what's the harm of a little worry now and then—especially if it gets us in gear to accomplish something in our physical interim?

Over the years at Murphy & Green, I've conducted an orientation session for our new lawyers. The challenge is to give the fresh troops a realistic sense of the focus and productivity a successful practice demands, without driving them further into the survival mentality that's already got them scared half to death. But one point I feel obliged to get across is that a due quotient of worry accompanies every file in our office. The discussion goes something like this:

> You may think the people at the top of the hierarchy have all the worries, but it's really the other way around. If there's a file I've not found time to get to,

my worry meter starts buzzing every time I glance in its direction. But the second I hand that file off to you, the worry, like so much toxic radon emanating from the earth below, migrates from my office *into yours.*

Now you'll be getting assignments from a number of partners, none of whom will be losing much sleep over how you're reconciling their competing demands on your time. It'll be your responsibility to deal with both the sensational and the relational implications of the resultant stress.

In other words, you must *feel* (stay conscious of) the pressure. In large measure, it's what keeps us on top of what we're being paid to stay on top of. But you've also got to remain conscious of your own needs and limitations. That means monitoring the impact, both here and in your larger context, of all we're demanding of you.

This, too, is part of good lawyering. And it can be a fine line between impressing us with your uncomplaining industry and having the good sense to say, "I just can't *do* all that you're asking of me."

I then wistfully tell them of the time, many years before, that Jack Murphy had asked how I was coming on a particular project. I'd responded, matter-of-factly, that I still had two other assignments ahead of his. As I turned to walk away, Jack stopped me. "Uh, Adam," he asked haltingly, "who's *worrying* about that file—you or me?"

"I'll tell you what," I shot back. "It's going to take me a week and a half to get to that file. If you want me to worry about it in the meantime, I can do that. But it's o.k. with me if *you* want to do the worrying."

Caught off guard by my *chutzpah,* Jack gave a confused shrug and walked away.

Now few other associates would have risked such impudence with the senior partner of the firm. But this was during my community days, when I was buoyed by a false sense of security. When the shit eventually hit the fan, I had to come to grips, once again, with the dilemma facing every other mortal being: Which files are mine, which are Jack Murphy's, and which are *God's?* How *much* worrying should I be doing, about what . . . and in what order?

I thus found myself relating to Murphy in a different way when he summoned me, not too many years later, for a meeting with an important client. At that time, the firm was housed in two separate buildings, about a block away from each other. I found myself literally running, briefcase in tow, from my building over to Jack's.

Struck by my own unseemly sense of urgency, I remarked to myself, "You're a 'grown attorney'—why so nervous about a meeting with 'the boss' and his 'important client'?"

Except that I was out of breath, the meeting was routine, resulting in a box of documents being transferred to me in connection with a potential lawsuit. I set the box on the rear seat of my car, intending to peruse the material at home, over the weekend.

A day or so later, I got a frantic call from Diane. "Something terrible has happened," she began. "I was driving on the parkway and the door of the car just *flew open!*"

Picturing one of my kids flying out, it was a relief to hear that the box of documents was the only casualty. "Your papers," Diane somberly reported, "are all over the Expressway."

Now these were original files, reflecting a ten-year history of transactions between the parties to the prospective litigation. They were irreplaceable. I couldn't imagine how I was going to break this news to Jack Murphy, especially after the fuss he (and I) had seemed to be making to impress this particular client.

With no pressing deadline in the case, I thought I'd wait for some inspiration (or lightning) to strike me. I didn't have to wait long. Within a day or so, Jack called to say the client was back, with some further thoughts he wanted to share with us about the case. This time, I walked, slowly, to Jack's office.

As I entered, he said: "You owe me a hundred bucks."

"A hundred bucks?" I restated. "Did we have a bet about something?"

"No," Jack drawled, "a hundred bucks is what I just handed Richard, here. He gave his own $100 to some *fireman* . . . who showed up at his **house** this morning . . . WITH THAT BOX OF DOCUMENTS WE GAVE **YOU** THE OTHER DAY!"

Years later, at a firm retreat, Jack and I were reminiscing about this incident. I reminded him how he'd summoned me to that initial client meeting—like some really smart nerd he kept on the payroll for just such occasions.

"If you need to show off for your clients like that, I'm willing to play the part for you from time to time," I assured him. "I just can't predict what outside forces might intervene to sabotage both our expectations!"

"And what *you* need to know," Jack responded affectionately, "is that I'm willing to do the same for you whenever you need me to." That's when I knew I really had "made partner."

Jack gave me one other gift that night. He thanked me for a conversation we'd had years earlier. "You know the one I mean—over lunch that day . . . in the *Chinese restaurant*."

20

Pills and Process

Some time in the early '90s, my brother Earl went through a personal crisis. I heard myself advising him, as our elder brother had counseled me, to see a psychiatrist. But in recommending the very one-on-one, professional relationship I myself had rejected, I was reminded of a story I'd heard at *satsang*.

A woman was at wits end with her young son, who only wanted to eat sweets. Her guru suggested she bring the boy to him—but not for two weeks. At the appointed time, the child was so moved by the guru's words, he promptly cut his candy intake by half.

Years later, the woman reminded the guru of the impact he'd had on her now grown (and healthy) son. "But I've always wondered, Master, why you made me wait the two weeks before bringing him to see you."

"When you first mentioned your boy to me," the guru answered, "my own sweet tooth was out of control. I needed time to clean up my eating habits before I could speak to your son about his!"

It was thus my younger brother's distress, rather than my elder's cajoling, that led me, gently but firmly, to my decision. I simply couldn't help but notice how similar my own eating habits were to Earl's.

It seems almost comical, looking back, that after a guru, a ghost and all the accompanying *mishoogas,* it took a simple look in the mirror of my younger brother's eyes to recognize and accept my clinical predicament. And to begin clicking the heels of my own ruby slippers.

I walk a fine line in so describing my decision to "get help" of this more mainstream sort. I've not arrived at Chapter 20 to recant the psychospiritual convictions I've gone to such lengths to relate. The fact is, I don't see a contradiction between them and the more conventional course I was now set upon.

Had I established the "appropriate one-to-one relationship" twenty years earlier, I'd be a different person today, but not necessarily a better, happier or wiser one. (And what kind of movie would it have been if Dorothy had clicked her heels three times before ever meeting the Tin Man or dealing with the Wicked Witch of the West?)

So I took the plunge and made an appointment with Dr. Blumenthal. I had met him briefly, years before, at the Jewish Family Counseling Center. I'd gone there in the aftermath of our break with Tanya and Sherman, and my caseworker had sought his input as to whether I should be on medication at that time.

But I'd come to that session directly from a deposition. After observing thirty seconds of my upbeat, adrenaline-boosted demeanor, Blumenthal pronounced me "not depressed." And that was the extent of our prior psychiatric consultation.

I didn't hold that against him when I was finally ready to get into treatment. For the next couple of years, he helped me take a closer look at those parallel personas (spiritual and worldly) I'd first discussed with Sarah. And my inability to find satisfaction, for very long, on either track.

I came to understand that my spiritual leanings were symbolically but perniciously linked to my mother, the nurturer. My ambitious side was staunchly associated with my father, the provider.

But his providence came at a Faustian price: Nightly, he'd rave that the greenback was God (and peace of mind, the *rich* man's booty). Setting no store in Dad's affection, I'd vowed to earn some scant respect. Someday, somehow, I would "show him the money."

Mother, not surprisingly, was Father's better half. Like TV's Mr. Rogers, she loved us just the way we were. "Life is what you make it," she chirped, "so do what makes you *happy*."

She was there for us at school events our father never came to. Still, I heard his muted groan beneath the weight of her good cheer.

Then, as I moved from adolescence into adulthood, Mother's focus took an inexplicable turn. She stopped inquiring about my vocal or religious pursuits and now began each conversation by asking how things were going for me at work. For some reason, this always felt like a punch in the stomach.

Blumenthal helped me see that I experienced such inquiries as a betrayal of the spiritual alliance I thought

Mother and I had forged. Her values were actually much closer to Dad's than I'd imagined. And it was a slippery slope from there to an even more devastating realization: that the two were no less aligned in his nightly atrocities.

So long as my psyche had Mother pegged as "good" and Dad as "bad," I was as stuck as they were in their relational homeostasis. I'd have to keep the values and aspirations associated with each parent at cross-purposes—just as Gerald and Abby had always seemed to bc. I thus lived in a state of chronic ambivalence, siding mostly with Mother's more "spiritual" paradigm, but with an undermining cache of loyalty to Dad's more cynical worldview.

Important as the above insights were for me, my "quality of life" was impacted less by them than by Prozac. This time, Blumenthal prescribed it for me at the very start of treatment. But it was only after some ten or twelve weeks that I experienced a remarkable and rather sudden shift in my emotional sensation. I use that phrase to convey that the improvement seemed to have nothing to do with my relationships *per se* or how I was conducting them.

Simply put, I felt well. Not the exhilaration that accompanied a victory in court. Nor the "blissed-out" state at the feet of the guru. This was an unvarnished sense of well-being, unrelated to any notion of earning *or* grace. It was like coming into some emotional nest egg—one that had been accruing interest all those years it had gone unclaimed.

The transformation was all the more astonishing for the fact that in the three months it took the Prozac to kick in, I hadn't been in any acute distress. It was as if someone had flipped a switch . . . and every positive thing in my life shouted, "SURPRISE!"

My ardent inner process seemed abruptly obsolete. Yet in my daily interactions, my energy was uncharacteristically robust. I was fully engaged. *Unconflicted.*

"What are you *on?*" Sarah asked, in a mildly accusatory tone. I'd just entered the foyer of her house, not having seen her for over a year. I didn't tell her right away it was Prozac she was sensing in my aura (though I'd brought the bottle of pills along with me). Indeed, I'd scheduled this appointment precisely to get Sarah's take on how this medication was affecting me. I certainly knew I was feeling better but still wanted her kind of second opinion.

Sarah, I should mention, is an organic health nut. She avoids not just medications but microwave ovens. Her idea of getting the day off to a good start is a glass of fresh-squeezed carrot juice—on a bold day, with a stalk of celery.

Nevertheless, after tuning in to these pills in my system, she conceded they were doing me some good. She added, somewhat grudgingly, that I wouldn't always need this medication.

I have my own misgivings about relying on a chemical to feel well. But there are sequelae of my emotional karma that haven't yielded to God's more spontaneous healing process. I'll continue to claim that healing with the fullest interpersonal and introspective conscientiousness of which I'm capable.

No less so when I say, "Praise the Lord and pass the Prozac!"

21

Insight vs. Healing

There was one aspect of my depression that seemed to stand apart from the more endogenous illness. As the extended family assembled each year for Thanksgiving, I'd sink into a lethargic state that would last all weekend. In particular, my mother's presence seemed to bring on a distinct emotional fog.

In the spring of 1989, I was shuttling relatives who had flown in for my first son's Bar Mitzvah. When I spotted my mother, down a long airport concourse, the degree and suddenness of my energy shift startled me. I dropped from a state of high intensity and anticipation to one of lethargy and depression.

Sarah had also come in for the Bar Mitzvah, so I asked her about this. She told me only that it had to do with some traumatic experience, when I was 10 or 11.

On another visit to us, several years later, Mother unexpectedly invited me to unburden myself of any criticism I might have of her parenting. This was shortly after my father had died, and I suspect it had to do with some grief counseling Mother was getting. (She mentioned she was making the same communicative overture to each of her four children.)

We were sitting out front, under a large elm tree, when she thus propositioned me. The truth was, I'd been keeping our interactions to a minimum that visit—trying to ward off the kind of tailspin described above. Now, Mother was asking me not only to stop the warding off but to immerse myself in the very energy that stood between us.

It was the incident to which Sarah had alluded that sprang immediately to mind. Around the time of my own Bar Mitzvah (age 13, not 10 or 11), Mother had left the house after a heavier than usual course of verbal battering. But instead of drifting off into his usual sleepy stupor, Dad went straight to the phone. I heard him say, "Hello, June? This is *Bob Schaeffer.* I'd like to see you tonight." He then took a shower, got dressed to kill and left the house for the rest of the evening.

For the next few days, I was caught up in a crisis of conscience and divided loyalty. Should I rat on my dad to my mother? Since she seemed the innocent victim of both his nightly abuse and this singular betrayal, I decided she deserved my primary allegiance.

Without batting an eye, Mother told me I was *mistaken* in what I'd heard. She actually managed a chuckle over the "misinterpretation." A friend of hers, *Joan,* was training to be a manicurist and had been doing Dad's *nails,* for practice. He'd called her (not "June") for this spur of the moment appointment. As for "Bob Schaeffer," that was just a stage name Dad used during his acting days at the Chicago Playhouse (with which "Joan," presumably, was familiar).

That night, I heard my mother and father yelling at each

other from behind their bedroom door. Only now do I realize how different, how much *healthier* this shouting match was than the nightly bombardments to which I'd long inured myself. How much more overt . . . and to the point.

At the time, though, I felt guilty—that I'd precipitated a worsening of my parents' status quo (disruption of their relational homeostasis, as I'd now call it). My father was especially distant toward me in the aftermath of the first real fight he'd had with my mother in many years.

Some days later, I was riding in the car with my parents. My instinct, even then, was to take initiative in the face of their communicative default. So from my position in the back seat, I searched for a way to break the ice with my dad.

At age 13, 1 didn't know how to say: "Mom and Dad, I feel as though I'm being blamed for the problem you two are having, and I'm upset that you've left me completely in the dark about this whole awful situation." So, instead, I said, "Dad, tell me about your days at the Chicago Playhouse."

"DON'T TALK ABOUT THAT!" my dad shouted at me. For the rest of the ride, not another word was spoken. For the next *twenty-eight years,* nothing further had been said.

As I now pondered my mother's unexpected invitation to address any emotional grievance I might have, the memory of these events flooded my consciousness. After reminding her of the incident, I took a deep breath and said:

Mother, do you see how you left me out on a limb after I'd allied myself with you in this drama? We might have taken some comfort in our shared (if quite different) aggrievement. Instead, you lied to me. Then you gave me up to the enemy.

And even after you and Dad had fought it out, you never came back to clean things up on my end. Or to reassure me that the two of you were trying to turn things around.

This was no diatribe against my mother. My words were soft and tearful. She also cried and, after only a bit of defending, took responsibility for what had occurred between us so many years before.

From that day forward, I've never suffered another depressive meltdown on coming into my mother's physical presence. That specific energy was dissipated by our belated but heartfelt communication.

I assume my remaining, more endogenous depression no less has its antecedents in specific (if cumulative) interpersonal experiences. Or in current relational circumstances, the full implications of which I've not yet been ready to address. Just as medical research looks for clues in any cancer cluster, so it behooves us to monitor our emotional fluctuations—to search out the linkage between our interactions and their psychosomatic effects. That is largely what psychotherapy attempts to do.

The healing with my mother also reminded me that identifying our emotional wounds and resolving them are two different things. Sarah had helped me connect the Bob Schaeffer incident with my ensuing "emotional allergy" to

Mother. But that awareness of cause and effect had afforded me no relief from the symptomatology.

In this sense, the thought and feeling are like twins separated at birth, each sensing their incompleteness. True objectivity, the kind that presages our emotional healing, entails both seeing and feeling interpersonal reality, at the self-same instant.

This experience with my mother also taught me that as long as I breathe air (and so long as those with whom I may yet effect some relational healing continue, themselves, to breathe), I must take my opportunities to resolve things with those who have hurt me . . . and with those whom I have hurt.

I was attempting to do that with my parents when I asked my dad to talk to me about "Bob Schaeffer." It just took another twenty-eight years for me to come up with a more artful approach. And for my mother, at least, to be willing to make herself vulnerable.

22

A Matter of Apples and Eggs

But how do we heal relationships with people who have died? Or who simply aren't open to process, however gentle and well meaning?

My father now fell into both categories. He'd certainly never invited any feedback about his parenting. In fact, on the one occasion I'd attempted such a communication, he called me "holier than thou." And left me with the parting benediction, *"An apple never falls far from the tree."*

I was contemplating that discussion some years later, on my way to work. I'd vowed that *this* little apple would move as far from the tree (and as fast) as it could thrust itself. "But how exactly *does* an apple 'thrust' itself?" I now pondered, while negotiating the morning rush hour.

I'd recently read *The Road Less Traveled,* by M. Scott Peck, and for no particular reason, it occurred to me that my answer had something to do with *Peck* . . . that if I'd poke around a little with this hint, the solution would become self-evident.

This kind of internal chitchat was a habit for me by now. It was a sense of impending insight—an urge to just stay with the subject, but in a relaxed sort of mental soft-focus.

So I meditated on the unlikely mantra I'd been given: "Poke, poke; Peck, Peck; poke, poke; Peck, Peck" . . . until the light came on:

YOU'RE NOT AN APPLE, YOU'RE A CHICK-EN! More specifically, a *chick,* growing ever more confined in its neurotic egg. From *inside* that egg, you can "thrust" with all your might, this way and that, but like the fallen apple, you'll never roll very far from where you began.

Yet if, instead of thrusting, the chick merely does what comes naturally—*pokes* and *pecks* against the shell of that egg—it will, in due course, hatch. And on that day (*bayom hahu*), discover things the apple will never know. Like *feet* (not to mention wings)!

I was so enamored of this "breakthrough," I called Diane just as soon as I got to the office. "You're not going to *believe* what I'm staring at," she said, after listening to my story. While I'd been meditating my way to work, Diane had been browsing through *Newsweek.* And she'd flipped, just as the phone rang, to this full-page illustration:

This portrait of me was part of an ad for an airline. It now sits on my desk, as a reminder.

PART FOUR

INTEGRATION

23

"Community"

The Road Less Traveled was one of those rare gifts that have inspired millions of people. I went on to read *The Different Drum; Community Making and Peace.* There, Peck attempts to distill the psychological and communicative elements that have allowed encounter groups to reach a collective, psychosensory state he calls "community." When a speaking tour brought him to Chicago, I got to talk with Peck about this.

I asked him whether positing community as a process-induced, group sensation didn't reduce it to a peak experience, as opposed to something that might be sustained and integrated into normal life. He invited me to follow up with him on the issue, and in a subsequent letter, I confessed I'd had my fill of such collective peak moments.

"Of what value are these weekend workshops," I challenged, "if none of us is willing or capable of achieving what you call 'community' in our ongoing contexts? And should we not be suspicious when our communicative zeal expresses itself not in the personal conundra of everyday life but in contrived encounters, with people we don't know and with whom we have no future?"

Peck wrote back, inviting me to a workshop sponsored by his organization, the Foundation for Community Encouragement (FCE). So much for having had my fill of collective peak moments. I soon found myself seated in a circle of about 25 people, in Knoxville, Tennessee.

From *The Different Drum,* I had a rough idea what was in store. In the first stage of community-building, the participants display the kind of sociable, performance-behavior I've described in Chapter 11. (Everyone acts as if they're already *in* the desired community state.) Peck calls this "pseudocommunity."

In stage two ("chaos"), the phoniness begins to break down. Somebody becomes impatient or otherwise confrontational, and things turn ugly.

By stage three, the participants start owning up to the fact that they haven't a clue how to get to "community" (or even much of an idea what it is). Peck calls this "emptying." Someone finds the courage to test the waters of personal vulnerability—to communicate without pretense or manipulative agenda. And this, like a drop of water on a parched plant, somehow allows everyone else in the group to lower their own defenses.

The final stage, "community," is that rare state of affinity (heightened sensitivity) that allows a group of people to stop performing for and judging one another. It's a collective state in which each person's unique presence, rather than his ideas or personality, is truly felt and unconditionally accepted.

Thus apprised of the community-building sequence, I came to the FCE weekend determined not to play the stage-two provocateur. But I was unable to restrain myself when a woman named Sherry, a veteran of previous FCE events, began describing the lengths to which she'd gone, over her husband's protests, to get to this workshop. Confessing her need now to obtain the community fix she'd purchased at so dear a price, she implored us to get on with the process —to move beyond the insincere banter of pseudocommunity in which we were mired. "We have only three more hours," Sherry somberly intoned, "to *make* it into *real* community."

"I DON'T GIVE A SHIT IF WE EVER GET TO SO-CALLED 'COMMUNITY'!" I heard myself erupting. "If you haven't achieved it in all the time you've had with your own husband, what good is this fleeting and artificial state you want us to induce at his further expense?"

So much for "pseudocommunity." Sherry came back at me with both barrels blazing. "YOU SON OF A BITCH!" she screamed. *"WHO THE HELL DO YOU THINK YOU ARE?"*

She continued to rail against me for several minutes, without let up. But I felt no need to defend myself. My experience in Tanya and Sherman's community informed me, irrefutably, that this diatribe belonged not to me but to Sherry's husband.

To be sure, my own issues had overwhelmed my intention not to play the instigator at this event. But I'd played it in a conscious if emotionally charged way. In point of fact, I'd accelerated the process, just as Sherry had requested (confirming the old adage, "Be careful what you wish for").

And as Peck had predicted, our conflagration seemed to work some catharsis for the entire group. For just as soon as Sherry's outrage had dissipated, we were quite done with the "chaos" phase and moved directly into "emptying."

The doorway was gently opened by Jan, who began describing her own marital dilemma. She was an FCE leader/facilitator (though not officiating at this event), whose husband was chronically depressed. Jan feared he was slipping away from her and that the two wouldn't survive much longer as a couple.

Unlike the thrust and parry going on between Sherry and me, Jan's statement was personal and straightforward. She was neither judging her husband nor masking her own distress. Nor was she looking to the group to solve her problem or, for that matter, even to respond. Indeed, it was the very unconditionality of Jan's sharing that was about to spark us into community.

One of the group's two leaders now asked permission to step out of his role as facilitator to address an issue of his own. Apropos of my point to Sherry (and earlier, to Peck), he described his frustration at being unable to *sustain* community, not just in his everyday life but even at these FCE events. He felt he was falling short of his calling, failing himself and those he was supposed to be serving.

This confession triggered a profuse response from an unlikely source. There was a salesman in the group, whose earlier pitch for "team spirit" (when we were stuck in "pseudocommunity") had fallen rather flat. ("Our group needs a *name*," he'd gushed; "like . . . 'the Peaches'. . . or 'the *Magnolias!*'")

But the salesman's new proffer was poignant and deft. He described his own routine, driving from town to town, persuading strangers to buy things they didn't want. He was starved for some honest to God communication. And so very grateful for the last fifteen minutes of it.

At this, the facilitator burst into tears. But the salesman kept right on facilitating: "However short you may have fallen, you've done me a great service. I didn't know straight talk like this was even possible."

The facilitator now began to wail in accompaniment. A duet, not an accompaniment—two souls expressing their common anguish. Experiencing the human dilemma . . . perhaps from different vantage points, but feeling it, *sharing* it. And allowing us all to share it, first through their eyes, then through our own.

As I drove to the airport for the flight home, I had a sense of openness, from my throat to my navel, as though my very guts were hanging out. For days after the event, I found it difficult to focus on the mundane activities of daily life.

We'd been warned of such a reentry phenomenon, so I was more patient with myself than I might otherwise have been. I wrote the following in an effort to interpret my personal state, and what I'd experienced in Knoxville:

1.   "Building community," as Peck calls it, means opening our respective heart chakras. That chakra responds, sympathetically, when someone else's heart stirs in close proximity. If the opening is permitted to continue, the group process accelerates, because our own sympathetic vibration now sets off someone else's vibratory network.

2.   *The risk of this opening is that it exposes us to pain we've been preferring not to feel. As the pupil of the eye constricts to protect us from too much or too sudden an onslaught of light, so we constrict the heart chakra in order not to be overwhelmed by our emotional pain. That's the gist of our defense mechanisms. (Only in this case, it's the "darkness" that constricts and the "light" that dilates.)*

3.   *Nevertheless, as a pupil fixed in the wide open position would more likely blind us than enhance our vision, so the heart chakra must open to a degree and at a pace compatible with our physical and emotional circumstance. The key, in both cases, is flexibility in responding to the amount and quality of the available light. This is what we should mean when we speak of "setting appropriate boundaries."*

24

Mutual Therapy

If the above attempts to explain the sensational experience, what, if anything, had we done together in Knoxville relationally? To begin with, Sherry and I wouldn't have taken each other's bait had we not each touched a sensitive nerve within the other's emotional network. I'll go so far as to suggest that Jan's subsequent sharing about her marital distress was closer to what was really on our minds, had we been prepared to address it. Instead, the two of us projected our marital conflicts onto each other and the group.

"Projection" is the tendency to overreact when someone else's situation or behavior threatens to remind us of our own, unresolved conflict. It seems we can't help but notice in others the faults or problems we've been avoiding in our own lives.

Now if Peck is right, this isn't a bad thing, at least in the group-process setting he calls "community-building." It was the very force of Sherry's and my own projection (the "chaos" phase) that seemed to clear the way for Jan to share her marital dilemma more forthrightly. And the fact that I was personally caught up in the exchange (what the therapist would call "countertransference") didn't make my gauntlet to Sherry less timely or on point.

As discussed in Chapter 11, reacting emotionally to the patient's process is something the therapist is trained to guard against. Yet it's sometimes this very self-monitoring that guides him to the real issue. By noticing when his own buttons are feeling pushed, the therapist actually intuits what is going on with the patient.

Now if, as Dr. Peck suggests in *The Road Less Traveled*, "any genuinely loving relationship is one of mutual psycho-therapy," the management of countertransference is something we must all come to grips with. For it's inevitable—indeed desirable—that we become emotionally engaged in our loved-one's process. A process in which we, unlike the therapist, have a personal and ongoing stake.

But "mutual therapy" is further complicated by the fact that the communication is a two-way street. Unlike the therapist, we're called not just to monitor our emotions but to voice them. And it's that very give-and-take that tends to bring us to the therapist (or the marriage counselor) in the first place. In short, it's much harder to *have* a relationship than to counsel one.

That said, objectivity and emotionality need not be at cross-purposes, much less mutually exclusive. What the conventional wisdom overlooks is that maintaining objectivity, once the emotional dust has been kicked up, is a spiritual, not a psychological challenge. It's about keeping the ego, not the emotions, in check.

Ego is the mother of all defense mechanisms. When a conflict erupts, it circles like a vulture, hoping to subvert the parties' will to communicate. And when it penetrates our emotional field, defensiveness is the behavioral product. Defensiveness is our neurotic stasis, energized by projection, then commandeered by ego. It is emotion gone bad.

Our very reactivity to someone else's communication should thus alert us that objectivity is, to that extent, *at risk.* But the interaction may yet prove a blessing, depending on what happens next. If we hand ego the reins, our relational work-in-process degenerates into defensiveness, sabotaging the communication. But if ego can be contained, emotion will *ripen,* into the same intuition on which the therapist ultimately relies.

In this sense, all emotion is nascent intuition. Intuition, in turn, is emotion, inuring itself to ego so as to attain its wisdom. And such wisdom—born of emotion, not intellect —lights the way to our eventual healing.

25

Addiction

I got a nice card from Sherry a week or so after the workshop. She wrote that she and her husband were going off for three days at a cabin on their favorite lake. "Now I know we have that time to reach community together," she added.

My own catharsis from the Knoxville encounter had less to do with my marriage than with an issue Blumenthal and I had been exploring. He'd pointed out an addictive quality to my pursuit of intensity in relationships—how I seemed to use interpersonal process to gain some temporary relief from my depression. I thus found myself wondering, both during the weekend and afterwards, whether I'd just fallen off the wagon. (This was the primary conflict I'd projected onto Sherry, the moment she displayed her own addictive craving for community.)

One of the most eloquent speakers at the Knoxville FCE event was Keith Miller, author of *The Taste of New Wine* and other Christian spiritual books. Miller's very topic was addiction, and he noted that one could be addicted to intensity, as well as to alcohol, drugs, food, sex or other sensations. He defined addiction as "any behavior that makes you feel better but isn't in your best interest . . . and which you cannot seem to stop."

Was I, then, the one palming process off as intimacy? The thought of so perverting my hard won insight was sobering indeed. I searched for a way to temper the addictive component of my own communicative zeal.

The answer I came up with was to monitor not the intensity of my interactions but my motivation going into them. Was my agenda relational or sensational? (Did it involve a "who" or merely a "what"?)

If it was sensation I was after, then I was using people—merely pretending to relate. But if my goal was truly to communicate (taking account of the other person's needs and interests, not just my own), I needn't abstain from all ensuing interpersonal commotion.

And of course, the subtlety with which ego insinuates itself into even our most well-meaning interactions would have ruled out total abstinence in all events.

26

Feelers and Thinkers

In the early, happy days of Tanya and Sherman's community, Mr. Dillon had a way of evening things up, so that whoever seemed to have come out on the short end of the processing stick would be given their due. This was accomplished by posing the question, "Whose gift was greater, Jesus' or Judas'?"

What Dillon meant by this was that without Judas to betray him, Jesus could not have fulfilled his purpose. Thus, when a consensus was reached as to who had played the "Jesus" and who the "Judas" of a particular transaction, the latter (assuming his energy had shifted) would be welcomed back into the fold like the prodigal son. Our pledge not to stigmatize each other was the ethical corollary of Tanya's assurance, during our first visit to the community, that "once the energy is resolved, it's as though the conflict never existed."

But we often fell short of that high moral mark, and I tended to serve, on such occasions, as the Pharisaic scapegoat. The collective judgment would be that I'd mortgaged my faith to some well-reasoned doubt; my love, to pride-driven propriety.

159

Many spiritual people tend in this way to play the "heart" off against the "mind." Faith and love are credited to the former, while the latter gets the rap for worry, doubt and having to keep our agreements. When Gurudeva Ji once had the misfortune of being sued, he commented that the law was "pure mind" (a most disheartening pronouncement for us few lawyer-devotees).

Dillon also occasionally bad-mouthed the mind, and I bought into this when I preached to my brother Frank that "the heart has more to offer." If I were writing that letter today, I'd say heart and mind no more vie with each other than do liver and kidney.

We had a version of this false dichotomy operating within our own nuclear family. When the kids were small, we played a game in which I would try to steal their "spins." The closest translation for this would be their "smells"; but what I was after was the warm, fuzzy sensation of rubbing my face right up against theirs—preferably, just as they were awakening from a long night of "spinning."

But when our middle boy was about 4, he started spurning me during these snuggling sessions, in favor of his mother. "What's so special about her?" I asked, in a stern but kidding tone. "She has love spins," came the reply. "Well, what kind of spins do I have?" I demanded. "Strong spins," came the answer.

———   ———   ———   ———

If the FCE workshop in Tennessee was about husbands and wives, the one in Denver, two years later, was about parents and children. There was Alfred, a therapist, whose father had been in the SS during World War II. No chip off the old block, Alfred was soft-spoken and conciliatory. Then there was Gene, who was bitter about his mother's parenting. "Her best just wasn't good enough," was Gene's angry mantra.

True to form, I again played the antagonist. For about half an hour, Alfred had been moderating our pseudocommunity, as if to fill a perceived leadership vacuum. When I finally called him on this, I sounded much more like his father, the Nazi, than I'd intended. The group leapt to Alfred's defense, declaring that he was coming "from his heart"; whereas I was obviously quite stuck "in my mind."

Henry, an older gentleman with some standing in FCE circles, eventually spoke up for me. Remembering me from the Tennessee event, he served as a kind of character reference.

Henry admitted that on first making my acquaintance, he, too, had felt threatened by my penchant for cutting to the interactive chase. Nevertheless, he now suggested it was the group that was stuck, in a picture of what "heart" was supposed to look like: permissive, not percussive; comforting, not confronting.

Temperamentally, Henry is more the conciliator than the antagonist, making him *Alfred's* more natural ally in this debate. Indeed, his defection to my side of the heart-mind divide had a paradoxical effect on me. Far from reinforcing me on the merits, it put me in touch with a deep wound—a grief I'd not previously been aware of.

It seems I'd been waiting a long time for someone to see beyond my strength and acknowledge my heart. Unexpectedly, tearfully, I began sharing my hurt over having been misjudged, on many occasions, by people who had made themselves "spiritual" at my expense.

As if on cue, Louis, seated just to my right, lunged straight for my wannabe heart. With a dagger my ego had slipped him, he denounced me to the group, as follows: "Adam's so arrogant, he sent a letter to Scott Peck. He thinks he's on *Peck's* level!" Turning to me, Louis demanded to know how many books *I* had written.

But the tide had turned, and the group was now poised to make hamburger out of Louis for attacking me in my moment of heart. Lucky for him, my impulse (uncharacteristically) was to head off the massacre. It was suddenly self-evident that Louis (like Gene's mother) was doing the best he could. So I asked everyone just to lighten up and cut him some slack.

I think by this point, we were all running out of steam, and the session petered out rather anticlimactically. But I left it feeling done with my karma as the personification of unloved mind. And glad to have relinquished the unflattering role in which I'd so long been typecast.

27

Relationship Building

Community-building with strangers, in a setting wholly removed from our normal relational context, can only accomplish so much. Despite the intensity (and sincerity) of our emotional outpourings, no piece of our ongoing life's work is present or at risk. Our families and bosses aren't there to test the reality of the love we claim to be sharing.

Thus, the dance we do at events like these should prepare us for something unattainable at the workshop itself. I'd call the goal sustained relational intimacy. In this sense, the workshop sponsor provides a safe environment ("a safe place to be in terror," as one of our Denver FCE participants put it), in which to practice the art of *relationship-*building. But it's only when we get back to our families and jobs that the safety net is removed and the real fun/terror begins.

One of the things I was mulling on my return from Denver was the difference in my energy *vis-a-vis* Alfred and Louis. As noted above, my reproach to Alfred had been harsh, even by my usual, unsugarcoated standard. It seems that over the years, I'd come to pride myself in the acuity with which I held other people's feet to the processing fire.

But when Henry's vote of confidence put me in touch with what was driving the acuity, it yielded to a less forceful, more compassionate self-expression.

As I replay this progression in my mind's eye, I realize that appearances to the contrary notwithstanding, none of my interactive dramas has been any less unilateral a *tour de force*. Behind the merits of my every fervent pronouncement lurks this unanswered koan: Does *Adam* (not his putative cause) finally have something he wishes to share? Is he ready, at long last, to be heard? (Or, as his fellow barristers might say, is he once again just "making his record"?)

The psychospiritual correlatives for this are:

Telling (Making the Record) → Sharing
Listening → Hearing
Facts/Information → Communication
Preaching/Teaching → Reaching

The left side of the arrow is more sensational than relational. And it's the relational quality of the right side that enlivens the interaction, transforming an intellectual or emotional exchange into a heartfelt communication.

I thought about the implications of the above for communication in my normal contexts . . . with Diane in particular. What was keeping me from seeing that my wife was also doing the best she could? If I could relate to her more right-sidedly, would her "listening" convert to "hearing" in response to my increased "sharing"? Wasn't that the Newtonian essence of the eternal soulmate theory—that a genuine shift in my energy would have to evoke the corresponding response in hers?

And what if the theory was just wrong? Suppose I made such a quantum individual leap only to disprove, once and for all, the relational hypothesis. Where would that leave my long-suffering marriage?

"What have you got to lose?" the nymph of my individual process reprised. "If you can pull it off (and live to share about it), will the relational impact any longer matter?"

PART FIVE

BETTING THE FARM

28

Jeffrey and Frieda

Most of our parents were suspicious of Tanya and Sherman, if not openly hostile. But Jeffrey Shwartz didn't have a judgmental bone in his body. He even attended a trance circle and was quite moved by it. "You sure lucked out getting *that* one for a father in law," Sherman remarked to me afterwards.

Frieda Shwartz, on the other hand, put the following on a package she sent to us in Normal:

ATTENTION POSTMAN: MY DAUGHTER IS CAUGHT UP IN A CULT! PLEASE PLACE THIS ENVELOPE DIRECTLY IN HER HAND. (IF SOMEONE OFFERS TO ACCEPT IT FOR HER, THEY ARE NOT TO BE TRUSTED!!!)

This was classic Frieda. And in the face of her histrionics, Jeffrey was careful never to raise a peep.

When the Shwartzes went out to dinner, the first order of business would be for Frieda to demand a better booth. Once reseated, Jeffrey would ask her what he was in the mood to eat. His passivity was the perfect complement to her bitter but more honest bite—like the sweet and sour she ordered when they ate Chinese.

I could write a cartoonish volume about my in-laws, had they not been, together, such brutal parents to my wife. When young Diane once froze up during a piano recital, Frieda berated her, right there in front of the audience. A few years later, an already fragile teenager made out with her first boyfriend on the backyard swing. Through a bedroom window, Frieda branded her a whore and a slut.

Jeffrey's response to such atrocities was unfailingly gentle. "My poor *boobela,"* he would say, with great but useless empathy.

I don't air these dirty linens to get back at anyone. The fact is, the events I'll soon be recounting would be inexplicable without them.

When we were in our late thirties, Frieda announced she had a serious family matter to discuss (in light of which she asked me to step out of the room). The bombshell was that Jeffrey had been married before. And Diane had an older half-sister.

Little Lori was only six when her mother sent Jeffrey packing. And he never looked back. But now, almost half a century later, Jeffrey's first *boobela* was flying to Chicago for a reunion with her father. It was, of course, Frieda who was finally spilling these beans—to "prepare" Diane for the meeting with her unheard of half-sister.

The neurotic irony of this goes back at least another generation. When Jeffrey was a teenager, his own father walked out on the family. Leaving footsteps for his son to follow, it was Myron Shwartz who first made his way from Brooklyn to the windy city. There, he and Jeffrey would both live out their lives, just a stone's throw from each other.

But Jeffrey never braved another meeting with his father. Near the end of Myron's life, he asked to see his son again and was rebuffed. This may have been the first time Jeffrey ever said "no" to anyone. Maybe it was his sense of loyalty to his mother (if not to his own offspring), back in Brooklyn. Just the mention of Grandma Clara's name always brought a giant lump to Jeffrey's throat.

Such striking disparity between the parents—one playing the perpetrator, the other, a hapless victim—is apparently quite common. As described earlier, my own family of origin had a similar charade going on. But I believe the self-deception was even greater in the Shwartz household. Diane grew up idolizing her dad, installing him on the very pedestal he'd reserved for Grandma Clara.

We'd long recognized the pattern of domination and submissiveness in the Shwartzes' relationship (which, to a lesser degree, we'd acted out in our own). But as much hard work as we'd done over the years, this revelation about Jeffrey's former life was our first real clue to an aspect of Diane's psychodynamics that had eluded us (along with Tanya and Sherman, two psychoanalysts and several marriage counselors).

Like her father and grandfather before her, my wife had the capacity to jettison what appeared to be close, familial relationships. Without missing an empathic beat.

29

Diane

Early in her professional training, Diane was interviewing the mother of a new patient on the children's psychiatric ward. The woman was relating an incident in which her young son had pinched her. Suddenly, as if there were no other way to convey the information, she leaned forward, took hold of the fleshy part of Diane's arm and gave *her* a prolonged and painful pinch.

Diane was so nonplussed, she pretended nothing untoward had happened. Her supervisors, observing through a one-way mirror, later asked why she hadn't responded to the assault (even to the extent of saying *"ouch"*). She could give them no real answer.

I suspect it was because young Diane's interactive life was no less carefully scripted than young Adam's. We'd both taught ourselves to repress our interpersonal discomfort so as not to have to deal with it. But while I looked like someone out of touch with his feelings, Diane's warm affect and psychological *savoir faire* portrayed a young woman very much in touch with hers.

Husbands and wives can learn a lot by observing how their spouse performs for his or her own parents. I remember being struck by the immediacy with which Diane would go into a kind of soft-shoe routine for her mother. It was a medley of pleasing, positive expressions and behaviors, calculated to keep the enemy distracted and at bay.

The "idea" of this defensive banter was to display total confidence and control, thereby preempting any possible criticism by Frieda. Like the scrambling device the cable stations use to make their signal unintelligible, Diane filled the airwaves between her mother and herself with a million bursts of positive chatter, effectively blocking the signal in both directions.

I don't blame her for this. The signal her mother was emitting was so critical and controlling, the only alternative to deflecting it in this way would have been to confront it head on. But Diane and her father had long renounced any such direct, confrontational approach in favor of an underground resistance. Their tactic was to display a cheerful obedience in the presence of the enemy's overwhelming firepower . . . while engaging in a lifelong guerilla campaign.

Unfortunately, we human beings lack the flexibility of the cable companies to scramble our communicative signals on a selective basis. We don't easily lower and reassemble our defenses to suit the diverse energies of all the people we encounter. Nor, in interactions with our most significant others, can we screen out their harmful spectra and let their remaining light pour in. We may be more nimble with those who've not gotten so far under our skin. But try growing up in Mrs. Shwartz's house and telling *her* about appropriate boundaries.

This habit of obliging chatter and behavioral niceness severely limited Diane's ability to establish a strong relational bond with anyone. For example, she had an aunt (Frieda's own half-sister) who was a regular visitor to the Shwartz household all the years Diane was growing up. Aunt Helen had a daughter Diane's age, and the two girls were frequent playmates. Their common grandmother (Grandma Susie) lived with the Shwartzes, so Helen and her daughter were always present at family gatherings and holiday celebrations.

But shortly after Grandma Susie died, Frieda told Helen she never wanted to see her *or* her daughter again! And as far as I know, she never did.

Some years later, I asked Diane if she knew how Aunt Helen was doing. "No," she responded with only token interest. "Well," I suggested, "do you think maybe we should stop by and say hello? After all, Helen hasn't seen our fifth grader since he was a toddler, and I'll bet she'd welcome a visit." "Good idea," Diane concurred. "Let's do that."

We had a pleasant enough visit, but it struck me that as willingly as Diane had gone along with my suggestion, she'd never have seen (or perhaps even thought of) her aunt again had I not proposed visiting her. How, I wondered, could Frieda have so thoroughly (and *vicariously*) purged my wife of all emotional ties to her aunt and cousin?

Much of Diane's individual therapy over the years had focused on her tendency to be, like her father, passive and compliant. She did dabble with some "assertiveness training" when it came into vogue in the late '70s and early '80s, but without any lasting effect on her anemic sense of personal authority.

When we moved to Tanya and Sherman's community, our relational tendency to have things my way suddenly came under intense scrutiny. For a long while, my strong spins were closely monitored, lest they even *think* of putting the muscle on Diane's love spins.

Within a few years after leaving the community, however, our marriage had reestablished its previous homeostasis. This was most obvious in relation to the disciplining of the children. Long after our boys were capable of contributing around the house, Diane continued to perform most of the household chores single-handedly. Between her housekeeping, shopping, cooking, chauffeuring and part-time practice, she managed to keep herself frantically busy —while the kids spent hours each day in front of the TV.

I'd come home from the office to encounter my wife's palpable but never more than simmering frustration. And in an osmotic process the mechanics of which still baffle me, I'd soon find "my own" anger at the children rising. Within a short time, I'd hear myself hollering at them for not being more helpful to their mother.

Diane's response to these remonstrations was invariably protective toward the kids and critical of my "harshness." The boys would then storm off to their rooms, angry at me. When they came back out, their mother would comfort them, and for the rest of the evening, I'd be the odd man out.

One day, I decided to try a different approach. I called a family meeting to see if we couldn't all pitch in and make Mom's life a little easier. We agreed the kids would be responsible for setting and clearing the table, and we'd each take a night doing the dishes. Diane expressed enthusiasm for the new plan and thanked me for initiating it.

But within a few days, a peculiar thing started happening. Diane would finish eating before the rest of us and begin clearing away the dishes. Her stake in the familial status quo was that extreme (and that unconscious). What she wanted, it seemed, wasn't to resolve her frustration but to continue channeling it *through me*.

Perhaps this was how she vented a lifetime of pent-up anger. Or how we transmitted to the next generation the legacy of our own childhood experience. On Diane's side of the family tree, I played the overbearing Frieda; she, the kindly but ineffectual Jeffrey. And on my side, I brought trouble home from work with me each night, just as my father had done a generation before.

It seems odd, as I write this, that the prelude to the present crisis would have been something as benign as the clearing away of the dinner dishes. But in the months that followed, I became hypersensitive to the dynamic this small incident revealed. It was, for me, a kind of wake-up call.

My relationship with the boys improved the more I abstained from their process with their mother. But Diane took my withdrawal as some implicit criticism of her (which, in a sense, it was). She accused me of never being satisfied with her "the way she was." And our debate over who was really judging her (and for what) created just enough friction to keep the home fires burning. A controlled burn, in lieu of the larger conflagration just over the next hill.

So here we were, down at last to the core of our defensive symbiosis. Our clinical trial of the eternal soulmate hypothesis was reaching its logical conclusion. If the theory held water, my resignation as Frieda's stand-in should create a neurotic vacuum . . . in which Diane/Jeffrey could no longer stand mute.

30

Smoking Jeffrey Out

What would have happened if, forty years ago, Jeffrey Shwartz had decided to be a different kind of person. Suppose he'd awakened one day and told Frieda he'd no longer tolerate her mistreatment of Diane (and himself). It's impossible to predict the outcome of such a confrontation, and no one can know for sure that any of the lives involved would have turned out better or happier.

But a generation later, I was determined to put it all on the line. I refused to serve, any longer, as Diane's emotional mouthpiece.

My sessions with Blumenthal were increasingly taken up with accounts of Diane's passive-aggressive behaviors, so much so that he suggested she get back into treatment. Based on what he knew of our history, he recommended Dr. Schechter. Diane, as always, was amenable.

I don't know whether Blumenthal had any such thing in mind, but Dr. Schechter embarked immediately on a psychoanalytic course of treatment, three times per week. I had misgivings about this, but now knew better than to inject myself into the therapeutic course he and Diane were charting.

For a while, the treatment seemed to go well. Diane would pause, mid-sentence, to remark that a cliche she'd just uttered was one not heard in years . . . one her *mother* had often used. Or she'd look in the mirror and be startled to notice her mom's skin coloring. It seemed propitious that she was finally identifying with the oppressor-parent (rather than the one who'd played the victim).

I should have kept that observation to myself. Diane passed it on to Dr. Schechter, who became indignant. Where did this lawyer/husband—himself the number one oppressor-suspect—come off making psychoanalytic interpretations? I was, once again, a meddler in someone else's "work" with my wife.

But I was not about to replay the drama of twenty years earlier. I declined Diane's invitation to vie with another analyst for the stewardship of her psyche. I did my best to respect a boundary she herself refused to recognize.

Then she started smoking marijuana. This had been a sore spot between us over the years, and resuming the habit at this juncture was her way of saying, "Put *this* in your pipe and smoke it." Of course, had she been capable of just coming out and saying (or doing) that, she'd have looked more like Frieda than Jeffrey. Her real agenda wasn't to get high but to get "caught."

I came home one day to find one of my old pipes lying on our back lawn, with marijuana residue in the bowl. Diane had called me at the office to say she was going for a hike at Black Hawk Arboretum. So I had an hour to think about how or whether to respond to the provocation when she got home.

My plan was not to take the bait. But I found myself incapable of interacting casually with her that evening, as though nothing was going on. So I asked her, "What's the deal with the marijuana in the backyard?"

Diane expressed total perplexity, denying any knowledge of the matter. It was as if to suggest that some burglar, having settled for just my old pipe, then tarried in the yard to get high. Newly mellowed, he must have repented of the theft, leaving the soiled pipe for me to find. (Perhaps the wind had carried off a note, thanking us for our hospitality and apologizing for any inconvenience.)

After reflecting on the unlikelihood of the above, I said, in a quiet but impassioned voice:

> So help me God, I'll not be your policeman or your prosecutor again, no matter what you do. I can't pretend I didn't find this marijuana or that I'm comfortable with you smoking it. But I can and do recognize it's not for me to decide whether you should or shouldn't be getting stoned. In fact, I'm open to the possibility that's something you may just need to do right now.

Diane looked me square in the eye and said: "I don't care whether you approve or *disapprove;* I have *not* been smoking marijuana. And I've no idea how that pipe got into the backyard!"

I teetered for a moment. She didn't seem to be stoned. In fact, this was the very self-assertiveness I'd been agitating for. Was I so invested in keeping her suppressed that I'd jumped to a logical but erroneous conclusion?

"Well, do you think one of our *boys* is into marijuana?" I asked, before making my apology. "I don't know," Diane soberly responded.

I called the boys into the kitchen, where we were having this discussion. I showed them the pipe and told them the ashes in the bowl smelled like marijuana. I asked if they knew anything about this, or how the pipe had gotten into the backyard.

Now it was my 10 and 11-year-old sons' turn to deny all knowledge of the pipe and its contents. I was utterly stumped.

Then, in a decisive departure from how I'd dealt with such impasses in the past, I truly did take control. Addressing myself to the boys, I announced my verdict:

Well here's the deal. I found this marijuana in the backyard. I believe Mom was smoking it, as she has in the past from time to time. That's not the end of the world. In fact, some people think alcohol is worse for you than marijuana.

You've probably also heard me tell Mother I sometimes feel more like her parent than her husband. I think what's going on here is, by arranging for me to find this marijuana, she's set me up to continue relating to her in that way.

I've just told her, and I also want to tell you, that it's not my job (*or yours*) to keep Mom from smoking marijuana.

Now let's go watch some TV.

31

For the Love of the Children

The above interaction was a significant event for me, my wife and my boys. For perhaps the first time, I had held my own with "Jeffrey," without becoming "Frieda."

Within a minute or two, Diane came into the living room, where the boys and I were now seated. She told them that she had, indeed, been smoking marijuana. She apologized to us all for having lied about it. Then she left the room.

When I mentioned this incident to Sarah, she called it a major breakthrough in our relationship. I'd now characterize it as a giant upping of the ante, for both of us.

Our relational homeostasis had been dealt a severe, possibly a mortal blow. I suggested earlier that what defense mechanisms are to the individual, the relational status quo is to the couple. That meant we'd now be finding out whether there was anything besides our neuroses to hold us together. Whether we were or were not "eternal soulmates."

I also learned from this experience that our children were the Achilles heel of Diane's neurotic complex. As adaptive as her neurosis had proved in the face of all the psychological, spiritual, individual, conjoint, conventional and quackish therapies we'd tried, what had worked, at least for the moment, was a direct but clean response to her manipulative behavior *in the presence of the children.*

Did that mean she loved them but not me? That she'd choose them over her neurosis as she was supposed to have chosen her eternal soulmate?

This certainly wasn't the first apology the boys had heard from their mother. In dozens of family meetings over the years, their parents' shortcomings had never been whitewashed. But Diane's foibles had always been passive —the kind of nonfeasance of which Grandpa Shwartz was so often guilty. Some regrettable omission or disappointing lack of follow through.

The real shift in the collective energy of our family was that Diane could no longer be Jeffrey without Frieda there to help her pull it off. And for the first time, she'd been shown capable of some Frieda-like *mal*feasance. She'd hauled off and *done* something "bad"—something in which no one else was the slightest bit implicated.

So the jig was up. Adam/Frieda and the kids were getting along together in the living room, love spins and strong spins commingling as though made for each other. And Diane/Jeffrey, though uncharacteristically the odd parent out, was at last fully present and accounted for.

She was off in her room, but energetically, she'd *showed up*. She was nobody's victim. And nobody was loving her any the less.

32

In Sickness and In Health

What did we really mean when we said, "for better or
for worse, in sickness and in health, 'til death do us part"?
If my wife of 25 years had become wheelchair bound, as
the result of some degenerative illness, would anyone feel I
was justified in divorcing her to avoid the anguish and
hardship associated therewith? Would it be different if she
suffered, instead, an emotional malady that deprived me of
sustainable adult companionship?

Ever since our early days with Tanya and Sherman, I'd
been committed to the eternal soulmate vision of marriage
as an arena for personal growth, fertilized by relational conflict and spurred on by the desire to preserve and enhance
the relationship. Implicit in this paradigm was the assumption that love truly could conquer all—including neurosis.

This had become, for me, an article of faith. In spite of
the disillusioning outcome of our involvement with Tanya
and Sherman's community, I still believed each increment
of individual growth brought with it, by definition, a greater capacity to love. And that the concomitant of one
spouse's increased love was a decreased capacity on the
other's part to continue inflicting pain. Almost as though

the latter, when all was said and done, would have no real choice but to grow.

I'd therefore assumed that the effect of each energy shift within the relationship was the reestablishment of the homeostasis on a higher level. And that with each such adjustment, our combined neurotic toxicity was diminishing . . . like an infection responding to a course of antibiotics.

But suppose the latest assault on my wife's defenses, however well-intentioned, was setting the stage for a desperate counteroffensive. What if her pathology, far from becoming less virulent, was only conserving its force for an apocalyptic last stand in defense of the neurotic fatherland?

Whatever the uncertainties, taking this theory of psychospiritual growth and relationship to its limit seemed the natural progression of everything our life together had been about. We'd soon find out, "for better or for worse," whether the extreme measures we'd taken to resuscitate our marriage in the early '80s (moving to Tanya and Sherman's community) had earned us anything more than another decade or so on marital death row.

"What a nice young man I met today," Diane mentioned casually over dinner. "You know, the one who stands at 44th and Stevens with the 'Will Work for Food' sign."

Of course I knew the guy she meant. Her bleeding heart made him a virtual toll booth for us at the intersection.

"Well, he was in the *7-Eleven,* getting a drink, and we struck up a conversation. His name is Mitch. It turns out he's all alone here, cut off from his family on the East Coast. The poor kid has a really good heart, in spite of a terrible family history."

Diane quickly found herself engaged in social work of the more traditional kind, networking with various agencies in Mitch's behalf. Within a few weeks, he'd been to the house and met our boys, our dog, our cat and our fish.

The next escalation came during a busy, pre-holiday afternoon at the office. Diane called to ask a favor of me. "Mitch has been getting increasingly depressed and has nowhere to go for Thanksgiving. I'd really like to invite him to spend the weekend with us."

I flashed on a scene from several years before. On the couch in our living room, Frieda had sat curiously clutching her purse. She was explaining how she and Jeffrey had first gotten together. Like Mitch, Jeffrey had no money and no friends or family in the state. Frieda had given him her phone number at a party, and a few days later, he'd called her up. . . from jail! (He'd let some tickets go unpaid, and the police had picked him up on a bench warrant.)

Now, in the suspenseful manner of a well-crafted closing argument, Frieda kept our attention riveted on her purse. Reminiscent of the sealed envelope in the O.J. trial, we wondered how she'd weave its contents into her theory of the case.

Finally, she reached in and retrieved her smoking gun. It was the tattered receipt for the bail bond she'd posted to get her derelict future husband out of jail! I'm not making this up. For 45 years, it had served as her license to dominate— proof positive she had no alternative but to lead Jeffrey around by the nose.

It seemed all too pat, but could my wife now be creating, in Mitch, someone who was more "Jeffrey" than *she* was?

Someone in relation to whom she might experience the competence and authority her mother had always monopolized? And was she also saying, "You want me to be more like *Frieda?* As you said to Sherry at the FCE event, 'be careful what you wish for.'"

"I don't like what I'm seeing," Sarah said a few weeks later, with real concern in her voice. As mentioned above, Sarah had been entirely positive about my handling of the marijuana incident. But her uncharacteristic pessimism, as soon as Mitch came into the equation, had an unlikely effect on me. I became almost smug. For some reason, when it came to this impending business with Mitch, I felt peculiarly out of harm's way.

There's tremendous irony in this. When we joined Tanya and Sherman's community, I looked back with embarrassment on the naivete with which I'd ignored all energetic warning signs leading up to my wife's prior infidelity. I was the man who said, "Sure, dance with my wife—just don't touch my car."

But this time, I was hardly oblivious to what was unfolding before my very eyes. This was not denial on my part but a deliberate bracketing of my emotional response. I was determined to relinquish all control over Diane. If the choice was now between surrendering to her neurosis (by retaking the reins) and letting it do its worst, my course was set.

"Sure," I heard myself saying. "Invite Mitch for Thanksgiving weekend . . . if you think it's the right thing to do."

33

For Better or for Worse

Day by day, I watched Diane blossom. The presence and initiative she was suddenly exhibiting, albeit in relation to another man, was a wonder to behold. Machiavellian as my clinical detachment may seem, my wife was emerging, as if from a long sleep. Not just behaving (or misbehaving), but *interacting.* As a self-possessed, autonomous human being.

And really *caring* about someone. I do not for a moment believe her attraction to Mitch was fundamentally perverse. What is our passion but compassion, spiked by the neurotic stimulus of our subconscious agenda? I was not about to suppress this awakening in Diane, mixed bag though it might prove to be, in order to preserve a marital status quo that had outlived its usefulness. "Thanks for the heads-up," I'd told Sarah, confident that if the time came for me to intervene between Diane and Mitch, I'd know when and how.

I was wrong about that. I did not know. Neither did Sarah.

Diane began stoking my suspicion, seducing Mitch and me simultaneously. Phone messages that were less and less discreet. Unexplained absences. What should "not taking the bait" look like in this situation?

I finally confronted her. "It doesn't matter to me whether you are or aren't having an affair with this guy," I lied. "Your willingness to push that button again, to play the affair card, is betrayal enough. It's over between us."

Sarah had suggested I hire a private detective. How odd that sounded coming from her. Like NASA, with its network of spy satellites, proposing an old fashioned, fifty-cent mousetrap.

"You miss the point, Sarah," I chided her. "If I have to entertain such an idea after all we've been through, the damage is done. What would photographs do for me, one way or the other?"

A month later, Diane made a suicide gesture. Her inner arms were smeared with blood as she held them out for me to see, like Christ on the cross. When she started running back toward the bathroom, our eldest son had to help me wrestle her to the bed.

Then the real illness showed itself. With no physical room to maneuver, Diane simply snapped herself back into performance. "It's all right," she said soothingly to our nineteen-year-old, like an outsider doing crisis intervention on someone else. "Let me go back in the bathroom and clean myself up. This was stupid."

"LOOK AT THIS!" I shouted to our nearly adult progeny. *"This,* not those scratches on her arms, is the sickness. Do you see what just happened—what she did to us *just then?"*

"I'm sorry, my son," I continued, almost weeping.

"Maybe I've pulled you into this situation because I needed someone else to *see* it. Not the suicide gesture. The *unreality*. I don't think I can bear this much longer, and I'm going to need you and your brothers to understand."

It was a Sunday morning, but it seemed appropriate to call Dr. Schechter. "Do you think she's dangerous?" he asked, for the first time inviting my input. "Extremely," I wanted to say, "but not in the physical sense you have in mind."

On the way to Schechter's office, I told Diane that after the session, I wanted a word with her and her psychiatrist. "That's fine with me," she so typically obliged.

After forty-five minutes, Dr. Schechter opened the door to his inner office. "What can I do for you?" he inquired, as he might have of the Fuller Brush man. I repeated the phrase to myself and counted to ten.

"I'm not sure," I replied. "But this morning's drama reminds me what an incredible actress my wife can be. I'm now wondering if she's even shared with you the havoc we've been going through as a family. Were you aware, for instance, that . . . "

"I can't say whether Diane's been having an affair," Dr. Schechter preempted me.

"And that isn't really the issue," I seethed.

"I *can* give you a referral for marriage counseling if you want one," he persisted.

"Are *you* nuts?" I wanted to scream.

"Here's what I'd be interested in," I continued, straining to remain civil. "Blumenthal has just retired, and I'm going to need someone to help keep my own head screwed on straight. I'd like that to be someone with whom you're on speaking terms—someone you have confidence in. Would it then be possible, without violating any professional strictures, for the two of you to confer? Or even for *all four* of us, perhaps, to talk?"

"That kind of thing has been done," Dr. Schechter conceded. "I suggest you go see Dr. Blakey. I did my own analysis with him, and there's no one in whom I have more confidence. I'll call and ask him to get you in right away."

34

The Psychiatrist's Psychiatrist

I had some wonderful sessions with Dr. Blakey, who quickly understood the implications of Diane's pathology —how it now had a gun to all our heads (including Dr. Schechter's).

"There are two things I really need your help with," I said to him. "First, I have to know, once and for all, what's the matter with my wife."

"I don't know why it's important to me. I'm not sure, at this point, it will change anything. But if she were experiencing physical symptoms as alarming as what we've been living through, I'd sure as hell be demanding a diagnosis."

That request seemed eminently reasonable to Dr. Blakey.

"The second thing I'm wondering is what I'm still up to in all this." I gave him the background of our experience in the community, my own family history, my work with Dr. Blumenthal, the guru, Mr. Dillon—everything. I also told him about Diane's home life as a child and her previous and current treatment from my vantage point. Then I described the events leading up to the current crisis.

"Your grasp of the dynamics at play here is laser-like," he complimented me.

"Well then, here's what worries me," I jumped back in. "What happens next if the process is allowed to continue?"

"That's a serious worry," he answered. "Her next step could be suicide . . . or some other dangerous drama."

"Should I give it up then?" I asked. "Are we better off separating?"

"I'd like to meet Diane before speaking to that," he stated, rising from his chair to signal the end of the session.

"That would be great," I enthused. "How do we arrange it?"

"Let me talk to Dr. Schechter," he replied.

"And about that second issue," I pressed on, at the risk of encroaching on the next patient's time. "Does the fact that I'm still with Diane attest to my love for her . . . or to the perniciousness of my own pathology?"

"Another fair question," Dr. Blakey acknowledged. But the therapeutic hourglass was completely out of sand.

35

Til Death Do Us Part

The phone rang. It was Mitch. Diane took the call in the kitchen. I stayed in the living room but could hear her side of the conversation.

He was upset about something, and my wife was soothing him. More. She was loving him over the phone. It was just obvious how much she truly cared for him.

When she returned to the living room, I was upset but not angry. "Look," I said to her. "We've both agonized over this situation with Mitch. I've even gone so far as to ask Sarah whether the two of you have done the deed. She said, 'not yet,' but suggested I hire a private detective."

"The fact is, I don't need a detective to interpret what I just heard. You *love* this guy. I'm not going to call that 'wrong' or try to put a stop to it. But why don't we just call this heart a heart?"

"Sarah was wrong," Diane responded. "We have gone all the way. I don't want to hurt you any further. I guess we should get a divorce."

I went to see a divorce lawyer. Diane called and made an appointment with one. Then she disappeared.

She didn't seem herself when she left the house that evening. But who was I, under the circumstances, to be giving her a pep talk?

When her mother called, the next day, I told her Diane had driven off the night before and hadn't returned. "Well, did you go *after* her?" she demanded. "No" was my only reply.

I was numb. There was nothing to do but wait. For the first time in our married life, I was the emotional spectator Diane had always seemed.

A day and a half passed before I bothered to call Sarah. She worried about a car wreck. "Have you checked the hospitals?" she asked. Once again, "no" was all I could muster.

"I have to put the phone down," Sarah said. A few moments later, she came back and announced that Diane was "out of harm's way."

"I don't know what they *mean* by that," she continued, as if questioning her own guidance. "I think she's at your old house in Normal—please call over there and have someone check."

I'd gotten no answer at the Normal house the day before. Somehow, it hadn't occurred to me to phone the neighbors there. They soon confirmed that Diane's car was parked out front.

"All the lights are on, but she doesn't answer the door. What do you want us to do?"

"Go in," I replied.

It was 45 minutes before they called me back. The boys

were asleep, and I'd been pacing around, imagining the most likely scenarios. And how I'd explain them to our children.

"There's been a suicide attempt," the neighbor intoned. "The paramedics are here."

"Is she conscious?" I asked.

"Yes."

"Is she coherent?"

"Somewhat. She's lost a lot of blood. We're going to ride with her in the ambulance; we'll call you from the hospital."

The hospital in Normal was a two-hour drive. I considered racing over there, but then I'd be incommunicado. And under the circumstances, I didn't want to leave the kids alone.

Our Normal neighbors called back and put the emergency room doctor on briefly. "We're trying to stabilize her," he said. "I've got to get back in there. I'll call you again as soon as I can."

I phoned my sister in Cleveland. The first plane would get her here around midnight. I told her I'd leave the door unlocked and write a note in case the kids woke up.

But I was still there when my sister arrived. The doctor had called back to say they were going to air-evac Diane to Northwestern Memorial, where a surgeon would be standing by. She'd gotten to within a millimeter of the jugular vein. It was impossible to know, until the surgery, whether she'd done permanent damage. But it was now at least safe to transport her.

I was there when the helicopter landed. Diane had a gaping wound in her neck. She spoke in the voice of a little girl who was the center of attention. She was smiling, almost bubbly.

"I *realized* something," she told me excitedly before they wheeled her into surgery. "After talking to the lawyer, I knew I couldn't go through with the divorce. You've always been there for me . . . and it's you I want by me now."

36

Be Careful What You Ask For

But did I want, any longer, to be the one by Diane's side? The Sunday paper had "Peanuts" on the front cover. It was fall, and Lucy was once again asking Charlie Brown to run up and kick the football.

"Sure, and what happens if you pull the ball away?" Charlie Brown demanded. "You could always *sue,*" Lucy answered. "She's right," Charlie Brown muttered, preparing for one more process with his eternal soulmate. "If she pulls the ball away again, I'll sue."

Dr. Blakey did eventually have a session with Diane, after which he offered me the following diagnosis: "Neurotic (severe), but not psychotic."

"She has what we used to call an 'as-if' personality disorder. This diagnosis isn't in the DSM,* but it was widely used some years back. It denotes an individual who lives her life 'as if' someone else's thoughts and feelings are her own. Looking at it from a systems perspective, you've had an 'as-if' family."

*Diagnostic and Statistical Manual, published by the American Psychiatric Association.

I flashed on a note I'd received from a congregant, just a few months before. Our eldest son had performed with Diane and me at a community-wide, Holocaust memorial service. "Our sincere thanks to you and your family," this woman had written, "for a moving rendition that enriched this year's *Yom Hashoah.* We survivors are especially emotional about families. And to see yours, harmonizing so sweetly, was touching."

Dr. Blakey confirmed that Diane's pathology went back at least two generations. "You've finally corrected the systemic part of the illness. The trick now will be to manage the system so it's minimally disrupted, while Diane works through this on an individual basis."

"Off the record," he added, "and knowing what I know about the two of you, I wouldn't rush to divorce her."

Sarah seemed of a different persuasion. She counseled that if I chose to stay with Diane, I should be prepared to accept her "the way she is." But she also held out the prospect of a more "suitable" partner, "waiting in the wings."

"I'm not done with this marriage," I told Sarah, apparently making my decision for the present. "At this late stage, I can't just cut my losses, call it a 'good lesson' and start from scratch with someone else."

"In the eyes of all who thought they knew us, Diane's gone from 'saint,' to 'harlot,' to 'mental case.' As far as I'm concerned, she's the same person she's always been. So if I loved her before, why would I stop loving her now that her neurosis has finally seen the light of day? Especially when *I'm* the one who insisted on 'outing' her."

"As for accepting her 'the way she is,' I'm not sure I understand the implications of that. I'm prepared to give up trying to force my wife to 'grow.' But neither am I going back to the pretend marriage we've had. There'll be no more holding ourselves out—not to our children nor anyone else—as anything but the broken relationship we truly are."

"From here forward, the picture will match the reality. If we can pull that off, I believe we can both stay out of further harm's way."

37

Dominion

At a subsequent joint session, Dr. Blakey offered us two anecdotes to explain a concept he called "dominion." The first was about his experience, early in his career, learning to deal with suicidal patients.

"What I realized," he said, "was that you have to be willing to walk right up to the edge of the cliff with the patient. But in the end, you also have to be willing to let him jump off."

"The gift of the therapist in this situation is his willingness to be there, 'for better or for worse,' when the moment of truth finally comes. This allows the patient to find out if he wants to live or die. But it also ends the therapist's vulnerability to blackmail."

"You, Adam, have walked that walk with Diane."

The second story was that of "Sir Gawain and the Hag." Sir Gawain was unsuccessful in love, so he went to the hag to find out "what a woman truly wants." The hag promised to tell him, but only if he first agreed to *marry her!* She then turned, magically, into the most beautiful woman Sir Gawain had ever seen.

Falling instantly in love, he proposed to her at once. "There's one catch," said the hag turned princess. "I can only look this way *half* the time. The other half, I'll be the old woman you first encountered."

"And I've got to be consistent," she continued. "I can be the hag in public and the princess in private. Or *vice versa.* But if you still want to marry me, you get to decide in which setting I'll bewitch."

To give reality to Sir Gawain's pending decision, the form of the would-be bride began changing back and forth, from hag to princess and princess to hag.

"I *love* you, my darling," Sir Gawain declared. "And I give that choice back *to you.*"

At once, the hag turned beautiful again—even more beautiful than before. "You've liberated us both!" she exclaimed. "By giving me my dominion—by loving me *both* ways—you've broken the spell that condemned me, *half my life*, to the lot of a hag."

"And to answer your question, 'what a woman truly wants' . . . is to *have* her dominion."

Epilogue

The *Shema Yisrael* (Hear, O' Israel) prayer, the watch-word of our faith,* consists of three paragraphs. The first begins, "Thou shalt love the Lord thy God with all thy heart, with all thy soul and with all thy might." The third commands us to wear fringed garments (today largely observed by the use of prayer shawls during religious services).

But the middle paragraph gives our Rabbi fits. It reads:

And it shall come to pass, if ye harken diligently unto My Commandments, that I will give the rain of your land in its season, that thou mayest gather in thy corn and thy wine and thine oil. I will give grass in the fields for thy cattle, and thou shalt eat and be satisfied. But take heed, lest your heart be deceived and ye turn aside and serve other gods and worship them; and the displeasure of the Lord be aroused against you and He shut up the heaven, so there shall be no rain, and the ground shall not yield her fruit; and ye perish quickly from all the good land which the Lord giveth you.

"Shema Yisraeyl, Adonai Eloheynu, Adonai Echad"—"Hear O' Israel, the Lord Our God, the Lord is One."

One Saturday morning, in the midst of all the drama described in these last few chapters, the Rabbi was giving a *d'var Torah* (rabbinic discourse) on the above. He confessed his discomfort with the notion God rewards good behavior with prosperity and withholds His bounty when we sin. This was contrary to the Rabbi's own life experience. And he felt patronized by it.

From my seat on the opposite side of the *bima* (dais), I joined in the discussion. "Certainly, God rewards the good and punishes the bad," I ventured. "It's the *application* that gets us into trouble. What *is* 'good behavior'? And what is 'evil'? What fate represents God's reward? And what His punishment?"

I then shared a story I'd heard at *satsang*. A king had a loyal servant who was an incorrigible optimist. No matter what happened, and no matter to whom, this servant would always say, "Whatever happens is good!"

This got a bit tiresome, but the king put up with it. Until one day, he cut himself shaving. "Shit!" the king cried out. "Whatever happens is *good,"* the servant chimed in.

"Guards!" the king commanded. "Take this insolent fool to the dungeon." The king then finished dressing and rode off to the hunt.

A pagan band suddenly emerged from the woods, surrounding the king. "Our god demands a sacrifice," said the bandit leader. "What better prize to offer him than the king himself!"

They tied the king to a tree and began gathering wood for a fire. Then they noticed the cut on his face. "This man has a blemish," the leader declared. "He cannot be used for a sacrifice." So the king was released unharmed.

Upon returning to the castle, the King recalled his servant from the dungeon. "My profound apologies," he humbled himself. "That scratch on my face did turn out to be a blessing in disguise. I'll never chastise you again for saying, 'Whatever happens is good!'"

But as the servant bowed and prepared to take his leave, the king's ego rebounded. "My slip of the blade may have turned out well for me, but it sure as hell didn't do *you* any good!"

"On the contrary, Sire," the servant replied. "Had you not sent me to the dungeon, I'd have been *with* you on the hunt . . . , and *I* would have had no blemish."

Postscript

An important corollary of "whatever happens is good" is that there are no heroes or villains in this story. The truth, as Diane had long recognized, was that I did not love her "the way she was"—as princess *and* as hag. That's what made ours an emotion-driven (karmatic) relationship—preventing either of us from truly allowing the other their dominion.

I still don't know quite what to make of Dillon. But he properly framed the issue when he asked me, *"Do you love your wife?"* And in the end, no mentor, dead or alive, could answer for me.

Diane and I stayed together another year, living in separate wings of the house. There was no further drama between us. And no energetic change in the relationship.

We had completed our karma together. We were not eternal soulmates. But we remain on good terms to this day, sharing custody of our two minor sons.

About the Author

"Adam Elliot" is a pseudonym. The author is a former law professor and leading member of the bar. He has also served as Cantor for a large Jewish congregation.

"Harofey lishvurey lev umechabeysh l'atzvotam"— "May our broken hearts be mended and all our wounds bound up."